Praise for Patrick Henry Hansen's

From Great Moments in History™ Series

"Patrick's link between history and sales is very entertaining, but more importantly, very relevant to modern sales and marketing professionals. If you are interested in dramatically improving sales results, read these books."

—Dr. Stephen R. Covey, author of,
The 7 Habits of Highly Effective People

"These exciting books of superb selling methods and techniques, told against a vast panorama of historical events, are not only entertaining, they also show sales people specific ways to double their sales and double their income."

—Brian Tracy, author of, *The Psychology of Selling*

"Patrick's use of history to teach modern methods of sales and marketing is remarkable—an inspiring, captivating read."

—Larry King, host, CNN's *The Larry King Show*

"Patrick's understanding of sales, together with his wit, makes his book series extremely enjoyable and informative. I've been lucky enough to see some of his ideas applied to a sales organization. As a result, pipelines grew, morale improved and our sales team performed better than ever. I strongly recommend his books and training programs."

—Kyle Powell, Co-founder, Novell

"Bravo... a maverick approach to sales and marketing. Patrick's use of history is engaging, interesting, and informative—a blueprint for sales and marketing success."

—Gerhard Gschwandtner, founder of *Selling Power Magazine*

"Patrick reminds us that those who ignore history are condemned to repeat it. His use of classic scenarios informs present day practitioners. He communicates solid marketing principles, helping readers understand the past in an unforgettable manner."

—Dr. William D. Danko, co-author of the best-selling, *The Millionaire Next Door*, & Chair of the Marketing Department at the State University of New York

"These are fantastic books. Not only are the sales concepts and marketing principles profound, but the manner in which they are communicated is totally unique. I strongly recommend these books."

—Hyrum W. Smith, Vice Chairman of the Board, FranklinCovey Co. and author of *The 10 Natural Laws of Successful Time and Life Management*

"Fantastic! If you're interested in dramatically improving communication skills and sales results, learn from the masters of the past by reading these books."

—Ron McMillan, Coauthor of the New York Times Bestsellers *Crucial Conversations* and *Crucial Confrontations*.

"In a word… WOW! An irreplaceable tool in the sales process, these books will make you a more impactful, learned, and skilled professional. As someone who facilitates management and leadership development, I found that the examples in this book even apply beyond the sales process. They are lessons for life. If only we all had the oratory skills of Winston Churchill, Mark Twain, or Thomas Jefferson. This book is a huge step in that direction!"

—Clark Jones, Corporate Trainer, Sinclair Oil Corporation

"Every day I have to sell my political opinions in the arena of ideas. Rarely does someone capture so many priceless truths of communication in such an interesting way. Patrick's use of history as a teaching tool is fabulous."

—Rob Bishop, United States Congressman

"Finally someone has organized and conceptualized the selling process. Loaded with historical facts, how to examples and practical strategies, this book is a step-by-step guide for dramatically increasing sales."

—Kurt Mortensen, Author of *Maximum Influence*

"Simply the most unique books I've read on sales and marketing. Patrick's use of history to teach modern methods of sales and marketing is informative and inspiring."

—Robert Dilenschneider, Author of *Moses: CEO*

ALSO BY PATRICK HENRY HANSEN

From Great Moments in History™ Series:

The DNASelling Method: Strategies for Modern-day Sales People

Winning Presentations: Strategies for Modern-day Presenters

Sales-Side Negotiation: Strategies for Modern-day Negotiators

Power
Prospecting

From Great Moments in History

Power Prospecting

COLD CALLING STRATEGIES
FOR MODERN-DAY SALES PEOPLE

Patrick Henry
Hansen

Second Edition

BRAVE PUBLISHING, INC.

Brave Publishing, Inc. Alpine, Utah.
All rights reserved. Printed in the United States of America

Second Edition.

ISBN 1-932908-09-9

This publication provides accurate and authoritative information in regard to the subject matter covered. It is sold with the understanding that the publisher is not engaged in rendering legal, accounting, or other professional services. If legal advice or other expert assistance is required, the services of a competent professional should be sought.

The *From Great Moments in History* series is available at quantity discounts. For more information, please contact Patrick Henry & Associates:

Toll-Free (877) 204-4341
www.PatrickHenryInc.com

Author Patrick Henry Hansen may be contacted as follows:
Email: phansen@PatrickHenryInc.com

TRADEMARKS

From Great Moments in History, The DNASelling Method, The SONAR Selling System, The SONAR Sales Cycle, Pipeline Velocity Reports, *SonarCRM,* SONAR (Strategize, Organize, Navigate, & Respond), TIME (Time, Investment, Money & Effort), and The Needs Resolution Matrix are all Trademarks or Service Marks of Patrick Henry Hansen, L.C. The superscripts TM and SM have been omitted for purposes of readability. However, the absence of superscripts does not indicate the waiver of any rights or protections afforded by those marks.

In Memory Of

❦ My father, Daniel McGavin Hansen,
who taught me the value of being bold. ❧

Acknowledgements

Special thanks to Matthew and Heather Moore for their meticulous editing skills, principle development, and insightful content review. Thanks to C. Parker Garlitz for his contributions and undeviating optimism. Thanks to my colleagues Brian Tracy and Dr. William Danko for their professional critique and personal support. Thanks to Larry Brooks, Darren Dibb, Kevin Dibb, Zac Fenton, Clint Sanderson, David Stephens, and Jason Walker—some of the most gifted sales and business professionals I know—for their insight and in-the-trenches feedback. Thanks to Bill Schjelderup for giving me my "first shot."

CONTENTS

Figures

Historical References

- Robert Bruce defeats King Edward II at the battle of Bannockburn. (iv)
- English and Scottish monarchs ban the games of soccer and golf. (1)
- Pentagon "experts" build the first fighter aircraft in the history of aerial combat without a machine gun or rapid firing cannon. (6)
- Isaac Newton discovers the laws of motion. (11)
- Gunnar Kaassen and his team of dogs deliver serum to the children of Nome, inspiring the great Alaskan dogsled race: the Iditarod. (14)
- Aristotle publicly disagrees with Plato and is banned from Plato's academy. (20)
- Nathan Rothschild uses Napoleon's defeat at the battle of Waterloo to enrich his family treasury. (26)
- President Kennedy withdraws troops from the Bay of Pigs. (34)
- Christopher Columbus gains the support of King Ferdinand and Queen Isabella. (47)
- Roman senator Cato promotes the destruction of Carthage. (58)
- Cleopatra conspires with Julius Caesar and Mark Antony to rule Egypt. (67)
- Celtic warriors battle Roman infantry using charioteer methods of warfare. (74)
- P.T. Barnum learns the power of creative marketing and becomes America's premiere showman of the nineteenth century. (76)
- President John Quincy Adams conducts an interview with a persistent female journalist while submerged naked in the Potomac River. (82)
- Johann Sebastian Bach, Wolfgang Amadeus Mozart, and Ludwig van Beethoven create the most famous music in history. (85)
- Leader of Denmark, King Christian X, defies Hitler and inspires his people to resist German occupation. (94)
- Francis Crick and James Watson make the most profound scientific discovery of the twentieth century: the structure of DNA. (115)
- Queen Elizabeth issues a political treatise providing rationale for intervening on behalf of Dutch Protestants in their war against Spain. (120)
- General George Armstrong Custer is defeated by Sioux warriors at the Battle of Little Bighorn. (122)
- Ch'u-Ts' prevents the complete destruction of Chinese culture from Genghis Khan. (131)
- German actress Hedy Lamarr files a secret patent based on information

gained as an anti-Nazi spy in WWII. (145)
- Meriwether Lewis inadvertently poisons the men on his expedition by proscribing mercury pills for venereal diseases. (147)
- Benjamin Disraeli outwits Parliamentary colleague and political opponent, William Gladstone. (152)
- Watching the doomed advance of the charge of the Light Brigade, French general, Pierre Bosquet lamented, "C'est magnifique, mais ce n'est pas la guerre." (It's magnificent, but it's not war.) (154)
- Southwest Airlines ignores conventional wisdom and revolutionizes the airline industry. (155)
- Michelangelo defies the power of God on Earth, Pope Julius II. (157)
- Bill Gates wins his first big contract with IBM by proposing 16-bit technology—technology he did not posses. (165)
- Mountain man John Colter is hunted by the Blackfeet Indians and narrowly escapes with his life. (171)
- Colonel William Travis, Davy Crocket, and a band of Texan soldiers die fighting at the Alamo. (185)
- Hernan Cortez and an army of 400 Spaniards miraculously defeat an army of 40,000 Aztec warriors. (194)
- Benjamin Franklin defends the character of George Washington. (203)
- Thomas Edison fails to entirely electrocute a man on death row using alternating current (AC) electricity. (211)
- Leonardo Fibonacci introduces the Arabic numerical system to Europe. (215)
- Moses receives The Ten Commandments from Jehovah. (220)
- British mathematicians and chess players decipher the famous *Enigma* machine to intercept German communication codes. (222)
- Peter the Great modernizes Russia. (229)
- Benjamin Franklin develops a self-improvement system. (231)
- Abraham Lincoln experiences nine political defeats before being elected President of The United States. (234)

For more information regarding historic references, see the Selected Bibliography.

Introduction

Edward I was one of the most capable and accomplished monarchs of England. He was also one of the cruelest. The line of succession for Scottish rule came into question in 1292, and Edward re-asserted English claims as the protectorate of Scotland. He appointed a puppet king who manipulated Scottish nobles with brutal political and military tactics. Building his power against the Scots, Edward attempted to subjugate the Scottish people by replacing the Scottish clan system with the English feudal system.

Three bold Scottish patriots stood against this tyrant: William Wallace, Andrew Moray, and Robert Bruce. While Wallace and Moray were the initial leaders of Scottish resistance, it was Robert Bruce who ultimately achieved independence for the Scottish people.

Bruce conducted sudden raids, night attacks, and scorched-earth tactics to torment the English. His repeatedly successful tactics rallied the Scottish cause and eventually forced a pitched battle with King Edward. Edward, however, died while leading his army against Bruce and his son, Edward II, succeeded him.

Edward II summoned a massive army to defeat the defiant Scots. He hired knights from France and Germany, infantry from Ireland, and famed archers from Wales. He bribed and lured thousands of Scotsmen who were opposed to Bruce into his army. Consisting of close to 25,000 men, Edward II amassed the largest army ever assembled by a king of England.

Bruce's army numbered between 5,000 and 6,000 men, the majority of whom were Highlanders accustomed to mountain fighting. They boasted no cavalry to speak of, but they armed themselves with something much more powerful than horses or guns. Aroused by English cruelty, the Scots' determination was fed by an angered populace.

As the English army approached, Scottish soldiers watched in amazement. They had never witnessed such a multitude of military splendor and might. In an act of desperate piety, the Scottish soldiers knelt in unison and made a short prayer to God, petitioning for help in the fight. Upon seeing the Scottish soldiers kneel, Edward II exclaimed triumphantly, "They kneel for mercy!" His aide de camp replied, "For mercy yes, but not from you—from God for their sins. These men will win all or die."

As the English vanguard began positioning its attack, one of its knights, Sir Henry de Bohun, rode boastfully to the front, clad in full armor and carrying a large lance in his hand. As he entered an open field on the north bank of the Bannockburn stream, he recognized Robert Bruce. Sensing an opportunity to demoralize the Scottish army, he turned his horse and dashed toward the Scottish king. Seeing Bohun charging toward him, Bruce wheeled his horse around and charged back. The two knights rushed toward each other in open battle in front of thousands of on-looking troops. Horses thundering toward each other, Bohun lifted his joust, Bruce his battle-axe. As they drew

near, Bruce suddenly swerved to one side and rose in his stirrups, bringing his axe down with such force that it sliced through Bohun's armor, killing the knight.

Stunned silence momentarily followed. Then, suddenly, a wild scream filled the air as the Highlander foot soldiers attacked the English cavalry. Inspired by the boldness of their leader, the Highlanders attacked with such speed and ferocity that they shocked the entire English vanguard into flight.

Even though his beloved Scots were outnumbered, starved, and poorly equipped, Robert Bruce led the Highlanders to victory. His physical courage, strength in adversity, resourcefulness in danger, brilliance in tactic, and unmatched perseverance won not only the battle of Bannockburn, but also the freedom of his people. Robert Bruce emerged from that battle to become one of the greatest kings in Scottish history.

Attributes of Great Achievers

Attributes of great achievers in history, like Robert Bruce, are not only motivating to read about, they are also similar to, if not exactly like, the attributes of great achievers today—especially in sales. High-earning salespeople demonstrate consistent personal and professional qualities that are akin to the achievers of the past. These attributes include: perseverance, tenacity, hard work, resourcefulness, overcoming fear, and utilizing intellectual skills and tactics. Although the *fields* of achievement change over time, the *characteristics* of achievement remain the same.

Prospecting is a mandatory selling skill. *Without* effective prospecting skills, sellers often struggle to fill their calendars with appointments and pipelines with qualified leads. *With* effective prospecting skills salespeople not only fill their calendars, they also pack their pipelines with qualified opportunities.

Power prospectors are intelligent prospectors. They think. They plan. They practice. They execute intelligent prospecting methods. They do not rely on luck to win. Instead, they deliberately place themselves in a position to be lucky. As Dwight Eisenhower's chief of staff during WWII, Bedel Smith, said, "Luck is where preparation meets opportunity."

Power Prospecting provides sellers with a structured process and clear methodology to generate leads and set appointments. By utilizing the concepts outlined in *Power Prospecting* sellers develop the confidence and competence to successfully prospect.

Note on Historical Content

> *Too many countries, too many businesses have been destroyed by not studying history.*
>
> —Donald Trump

George Santayana said, "Those who cannot remember the past are condemned to repeat it." Oliver Wendell Holmes, Jr., remarked, "A page of history is worth a volume of logic." Cicero observed, "To be ignorant of what happened before you were born is to remain forever a child." Most of us hear these quotes from time to time; nevertheless, how many of us actually recall specific lessons from the past and apply them to our personal and business lives? We know of Rome's decadence, the French aristocracy's arrogance, and Stalin's brutality, but what can we learn from this knowledge that can help us in business and negotiation?

Actually, quite a lot. Behind these events are great lessons of history. Whether they are small or epic, history's stories provide instruction of immense importance.

Nothing beats personal experience, of course, but learning from others' experiences comes in a competent second. The risk in learning only from personal experience is that too often, we draw conclusions from too little data—we learn too much from too little.

Because history is such an excellent teacher, I reference numerous historical events throughout this book. Every chapter in each of the *From Great Moments in History* series begins with an historic event that illustrates a particular point or principle. These lessons and events are worth learning precisely because they teach something of value.

The SONAR Selling System

Early in my career, I focused on acquiring sales skills. I participated in trainings, read books, and attended seminars. Most importantly, I made sales. However, as my experience grew, I recognized that sales skills were not enough. I learned that selling is a comprehensive endeavor that includes prospecting, investigating, presenting, negotiating, and lead tracking capabilities.

The SONAR Selling System

Figure I.1

Over the years, I created a systematic approach to selling that encompasses all of the skills and processes needed to become a successful seller. Called *The SONAR Selling System,* this logical, holistic approach includes prospecting, investigating, presenting, and negotiating skills. Coupled with sales automation/CRM technology and effective marketing, *The SONAR Selling System* equips individuals and organizations with the skills, strategies, and processes to win more sales.

The SONAR Selling System is an orderly, validated approach to selling. It is a system that has been tested extensively in a wide variety of markets, industries, and cultures. It works. By using *The SONAR Selling System* and mastering the skills associated with each step of the sales cycle, sellers stand out from the thousands of average salespeople who sell on *instinct* instead of *intellect.*

Integrity: The Foundation of Power Prospecting

A young Englishman searching for the secret of success sought the advice of a wealthy businessman in London.

"Go over to the window, look out, and tell me what you see," said the businessman.

"I see the marketplace," the youth replied.

"Now go look into the mirror and tell me what you see."

"Well, naturally, I see myself."

"In each case you were looking through a pane of glass. Tell me, what is the difference?" the businessman asked.

"The window is a clear pane of glass that allows me to see out and see the people in the marketplace. The mirror has a backing of silver that reflects my image."

"Therein lies the secret of success: When you let silver come between you and the people in the marketplace, you are only going to see yourself."

Power Prospecting is not a program of clever gimmicks or manipulative techniques. It is a system based on values, trust, and integrity. It is a *customer-centered* system designed to help salespeople stop thinking in terms of products and features, and start thinking in terms of buyer needs, goals, and objectives. Using power prospecting principles salespeople develop meaningful relationships and advance buyers through the sales cycle using honest, effective selling strategies.

Selling with integrity is not only the right thing to do, it is the smart thing to do. Because buyers make assessments about the character and integrity of sellers, it is imperative to demonstrate honesty and integrity throughout the sales process. Buyers need to know that sellers are trustworthy. "Am I dealing with Vinny the back slapping, plaid-jacketed, used-car salesman trying to sell me a pink Yugo, or is this someone I can trust?" As the great sales educator Zig Ziglar says, "The most important persuasion tool you have in your entire arsenal is integrity." Without integrity, salespeople severely limit their ability to establish honest rapport and build long-term relationships with clients.

Note on References

The SONAR Sales Cycle consists of four steps, each step requiring a different skill set. To help salespeople master each skill set, *Patrick Henry & Associates* provides training programs and books that specifically address each stage of the selling process:

Sales Cycle	Book Title
1. Prospecting	*Power Prospecting*
2. Investigating	*The DNASelling Method*
3. Presenting	*Winning Presentations*
4. Closing	*Sales-Side Negotiation*

Because each step of the sales cycle is part of an overall process rather than an isolated event, all of the books in the *From Great Moments in History* series reference each other in footnotes. Combined, the books offer sellers and managers a reference library that addresses each step in the selling process.[1]

---

1. For more information about *The DNASelling Method, Winning Presentations, and Sales-Side Negotiation* visit www.Amazon.com or www.PatrickHenryInc.com.

Note on Format

Power Prospecting contains self-study questions that facilitate the implementation of power prospecting concepts. Where there is a need for special emphasis, one of three alert windows is used:

> **Note:** A "Note" is an idea, concept, or principle that is highlighted for clarity and impact.

> **Caution!** The "Caution" window makes sellers aware of potential prospecting mistakes to avoid.

> **The Point?** "The Point" focuses the reader on the prominent principle or main idea of the section or chapter.

Thank you for your interest in promoting and exercising *Power Prospecting* strategies. I hope you will draw upon your own experiences to personalize and adapt the material to fit your own business or situation.

Please contact *Patrick Henry & Associates* with any questions or comments you have about learning *Power Prospecting* principles. We encourage you to share with us your comments, questions, and experiences.

Best Regards.

Patrick Henry Hansen

Patrick Henry Hansen

part one

PRE-PROSPECTING PREPARATION

CHAPTER 1

Power Prospecting

*Two horses were carrying two loads. The front Horse went well,
but the rear Horse was lazy. The men began to pile the rear Horse's
load on the front Horse; when they had transferred it all, the rear
Horse found it easy going, and he said to the front Horse: "Toil
and sweat! The more you have to suffer." When they reached the
tavern, the owner said, "Why should I fodder two horses when I
carry all on one? I had better give the one all the food it wants,
and cut the throat of the other; at least I shall have the hide. And
so he did.*

—Leo Tolstoy, *Fables*

In 1314, English King Edward II issued a royal edict banning the game of soccer. "We command and forbid on behalf of the King, on pain of imprisonment, such game to be used." In 1491, King James IV of Scotland banned golf. "It is statute and ordained that in no place of the Realm there be used... golf, or other unprofitable sports."

Although criticized for their edicts, there was a reason for the bans. The kings considered non-military related sports "unprofitable" because they were distracting young men from archery practice, swordsmanship, and other training necessary to the defense of their countries. Without a populace of trained archers and swordsmen, they would be unable to raise an effective army in times of crisis.

Like medieval celts and saxons, many salespeople are distracted from focusing on activities that build long term success—and no activity has more of an effect on a salesperson's long term success than prospecting.

While other selling activities are considered more enticing, prospecting is the foundation of any high performance sales career.

I managed an extremely talented salesperson who had the personality, charm, and brains to become an exceptional sales professional. There was just one problem: he refused to cold call. He viewed prospecting as an activity that only entry-level sellers engaged in. He was "above" cold calling. Since he inherited a territory with a bulked-up pipeline, he saw no need to "waste" his time on trivial cold calling activities. In fact, just prior to my appointment as vice president of sales, he was awarded the prestigious *salesperson of the year award*. He could do no wrong.

I immediately predicted what was going to happen and warned him that he was falling into one of the most common of all sales traps. I informed him that even the most rookie sellers would pass him by if he didn't continually replenish his pipeline with qualified leads. Ignoring my warnings, he continued focusing on a limited number of large accounts without simultaneously generating new leads.

Within a year, my prediction came true, and the most recently hired salespeople with limited product knowledge and sales experience passed him in revenue generation. As of this writing, the four novice salespeople are still the top sellers for that company. By following intelligent pipeline management principles and implementing cerebral prospecting skills, they continue to qualify accounts, set appointments, and generate revenue on a consistent basis. (For a detailed review of effective pipeline management, definitions, and processes, see Chapter 3).

Like the horse in Tolstoy's fable, salespeople can get away with not prospecting for a while, but it will eventually catch up with them. The salespeople who continually prospect are the salespeople who are rewarded the most.

> **The Point?** Effective prospecting skills are at the heart of successful selling. Sellers who consistently generate qualified leads and appropriately manage pipelines make more sales.

The SONAR Sales Cycle

As mentioned in the introduction, *The SONAR Sales Cycle* has four stages:

1. Prospecting
2. Investigating
3. Presenting
4. Closing

Each stage of the sales cycle has its own process and accompanying selling behaviors. For example, the prospecting stage of the sales cycle focuses on lead generation, cold calling, qualifying, client introductions, and initial appointments. Each selling stage requires specific skills and behaviors that address the issues at hand. But the objective of each stage of the sales cycle is the same: *advance the sale to the next stage of the sales cycle.* The only way to measure success is if a sale advances from one stage of the sales cycle to the next.

Selling is a process. It has a beginning, a middle, and an end. By ignoring the natural evolution of a sale and engaging in the wrong sales behavior at the wrong time, sellers won't reach their full potentials. For instance, if sellers immediately jump from the prospecting stage of the sales cycle to the closing stage of the sales cycle, they will miss vital selling steps such as discovering critical needs, identifying problems, or building value prior to presenting.

As the first step of the sales cycle, prospecting is the beginning of the sales process and has an enormous impact on a seller's success. The quantity and quality of prospecting results determine the volume and caliber of sales a professional makes.

The number one reason many salespeople fall short of reaching their full potential is not having enough qualified leads. Unsuccessful sellers don't generate enough qualified opportunities to maintain or sustain growth because they don't deal with enough prospects who have the willingness or ability to buy. Without an adequate supply of qualified accounts, even sellers with excellent selling skills are not successful.

The SONAR Sales Cycle

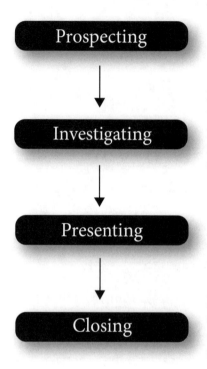

Lead generation, cold calling, obtaining referrals, initial meetings, discovery-qualification questions.

Information gathering, questioning, understanding buyer needs and problems, identifying primary buying motives, need-problem questions, ascertain-pain questions.

Presenting capabilities, demonstrating value, proposing solutions, submitting proposals, providing references.

Preventing and overcoming objections, following up, gaining commitment, obtaining agreement, negotiating.

Figure 1.1

The number two reason many salespeople don't reach their full potential is closely related to the first: poor pipeline management.[1] Similar in principle to poor cash flow management in accounting, ineffective pipeline management leads to unsuccessful sellers. These sellers often stay busy closing major accounts and serving existing clients without simultaneously generating new accounts. Later, when the major accounts close, they scramble to "scrape up" new sales. Unfortunately, far too often, their actions are too late. The traditional valleys of selling sometimes turn into gaping chasms.

---

1. See Chapter 3 for more information regarding pipeline management, terminology, and reporting.

Without good pipeline management and a consistent flow of qualified leads, even the most skilled sales professionals struggle to succeed.

> **The Point?** "As ye sow, so shall ye reap" (Galatians 6:7). Healthy sales pipelines reflect the law of the harvest. Sellers who generate sufficient qualified leads and manage their pipelines appropriately reap what they sow: sales.

Prospecting Versus Marketing

Many businesses and sales organizations confuse prospecting activities with marketing activities—they are not the same. *Prospecting strategies attempt to directly contact potential buyers; whereas, marketing strategies encourage potential buyers to contact you.* Understanding the distinction is critical because the strategies involve different activities and use dissimilar tactics to achieve their purposes.

Marketing is also not the same as selling. Using the broadest definition, sales is about fulfilling the demand that marketing generates. When done appropriately, marketing is a multi-disciplinary function that involves corporate and product brand management, analysis of both competitor and customer preferences, market segmentation, and advertising.

Specific marketing activities include:

- Competitor analysis and customer research
- Magazine, print, and publication advertisements
- Radio and television advertisements
- Web Site advertisements
- Yellow Page advertisements
- Billboard advertisements
- Internet marketing
- Brochure creation and distribution
- Newsletter circulation
- Direct mail campaigns

Some endeavors that appear to be prospecting activities are actually marketing functions. For example, using pay-per-click search engine submissions to drive qualified traffic to your Web site is a fantastic way to generate new leads; however, it is not a prospecting activity. It is a marketing activity, a method that attempts to get buyers to *contact you* via the Internet, not the other way around.[2]

The Top Three Methods for Prospecting

In the 1960s, Pentagon experts concluded that aerial combat in the future would only be fought from a great distance. Airplanes would fly at supersonic speeds, radar would see the enemy, missiles would be launched from great distances, and battles would be won and lost by pilots who never saw the enemy planes. The Air Force engineers and military experts were so certain that close range dogfighting was antiquated that they built the first fighter aircraft in the history of aerial combat that was not equipped with a machine gun or rapid firing cannon—the F-4 Phantom.

Over North Vietnam, their decision proved disastrous. The F-4 Phantom was defenseless against the lighter, more versatile Soviet MiGs. The MiGs would maneuver at close range where the American missiles weren't effective and shoot down the bigger, less maneuverable and *gunless* F-4. The decision to build combat airplanes without machine guns was a tragic mistake for many of America's finest young men.

---

2. For more information regarding pay-per-click and other effective Internet marketing strategies, contact *Patrick Henry & Associates, Inc.* at 1 (877) 204-4341 or visit www.PatrickHenryInc.com.

Like the Pentagon experts who considered aerial dogfighting to be a thing of the past, many sales "experts" casually dismiss cold calling as an archaic means of generating qualified accounts. They claim that cold calling represents a primitive approach to selling practiced by old school salespeople. Unfortunately, like the F-4 Phantom debacle, salespeople who neglect to utilize validated prospecting strategies, including cold calling, will be outmaneuvered and shot down by less naïve and more savvy competitors.

Highly successful salespeople and sales organizations employ numerous prospecting methods to find new customers. These methods include:

- Networking at social functions
- Interacting at chamber of commerce meetings
- Attending trade shows
- Getting involved in community organizations
- Conducting seminars

Obviously, not all prospecting activities are equal. When I first started my sales consultation business, I joined the local chamber of commerce and attended one of their networking functions where I exchanged business cards and brochures with dozens of attendees. Seasoned chamber of commerce members swarmed to get my business as a new member. I had insurance agents, financial advisers, printing representatives, and other salespeople calling my cell phone, office phone and even my home phone. I spent the next month dodging salespeople attempting to sell goods and services to me! The experience proved to be so time consuming and useless that I was embarrassed to have attended the event.

While the aforementioned prospecting activities can be worthwhile for particular sellers in specific industries, the three most consistent and effective prospecting methods remain:

1. Asking For Referrals
2. Executive Networking
3. Cold Calling

Asking For Referrals

There is nothing unconventional about asking for referrals, except that no one does it. When was the last time a salesperson asked you for a referral?

Asking for referrals is one of the most powerful ways to generate qualified leads; in fact, leads obtained from satisfied customers are almost always more qualified than leads generated from other prospecting sources. The close ratio on a pre-qualified, referred lead is invariably higher than a lead from any other source.

Research shows that referrals strengthen direct communication with prospects more than any other method. Beginning a sales conversation with, "Hi Ms. Thompson. Jerry Peterson suggested that I call you" is the best way to begin a buyer-seller relationship.

Referrals also differentiate you from competitors and give you an edge. If out of six cold calls to your potential buyer, you are the only one who can say, "Your colleague, Susan, informs me that you've been investigating new CRM software and that I may be of service," you have an advantage. You are offering your help at the suggestion of the buyer's friend. Referencing a buyer's colleague makes it much harder for him or her to toss you aside into the "send me a brochure" pile.

Sellers have nothing to lose and everything to gain by asking for referrals. With that said, why do many sales professionals overlook this opportunity? There are many reasons, but the most common reason is forgetfulness. Many salespeople simply forget to ask buyers for referrals.

Sellers need to make asking for referrals a part of their selling *modus operandi* by keeping in mind that:

1. Referred prospects represent a higher-quality lead than non-referred prospects.
2. Referred prospects are more likely to meet with sellers than non-referred prospects.
3. Referred prospects are statistically more inclined to purchase proposed products and services.

Referrals are the most potent form of new sales leads, but they seldom happen without effort. After a sale is made, sellers should make polite, professional requests for leads and referrals. For example, a seller might ask a new customer, "Ms. Taylor, do you know of anyone else in your company or industry who might benefit from our product?" Or, "Jim, is there anyone else who might be interested in using our service?" The key is to solicit the assistance of new clients who are excited about their recent purchase.

Once a referral has been provided, be sure to send thank-you notes, emails, and/or letters to the person who provided the referral. You might reward customers who provide referrals with gift certificates, credits, extensions, or other incentives. The well-rewarded customer will look forward to your calls and visits. I've had customers actually call me to ask how they may be of help. Wow! Think of the folly of not tapping into this resource of satisfied, happy customers.

The Point? Don't underestimate the power of a referral from a satisfied customer. Make asking for referrals a standard part of your prospecting activities.

Executive Networking

There are two challenges all sales professionals face when prospecting:

1. Getting through to ultimate decision-makers
2. Establishing trust and credibility with buyers

Executive networking (sometimes referred to as reference selling) overcomes both challenges. By having a satisfied customer call a prospect as an "account sponsor," sellers increase the likelihood of getting through to ultimate decision-makers on the first call because it's not a solicitation call; it's a testimonial call. Because the sponsor is a third party and has a title similar to the potential buyer, there is an immediate bond of credibility and trust.

Executive networking is one of the most available yet underutilized prospecting methods that exists. I often ask training participants to raise their hands if they have satisfied customers in their territory. Next, I ask them how many satisfied customers they have. Participants usually answer, "I'd say at least ten, maybe more." "Forty-five." "Twenty-six." "Hundreds." O.K.—so far, so good. We then ask them to keep their hands in the air if they have ever used even one of their satisfied customers to make a call on their behalf. The fact that ninety percent of the hands go down, never surprises me, but always amazes me.

Because most executives refuse to take solicitation calls, sellers find it difficult to start at the top of the business chain without employing nontraditional selling strategies. Existing client executives or satisfied customers calling on your behalf is both an effective and unconventional way to access top executives and decision-makers.

One of the reasons executive networking is so effective is that it has the dual effect of being both a sales call and a testimonial call. This provides an opportunity for sellers to open the call at the highest echelons of an organization with power and credibility.

If some executives are more inclined to send a letter or email than to make a telephone call, that's fine. Use the executive networking letter or email as a springboard to contact the buyer and set up an appointment.

Sellers need to provide incentives for the satisfied customer who is making the prospecting call. For instance, a seller might send the person making the call a gift certificate or a discount on a future purchase—some type of reward for making the call.

The Point? Executive-to-executive calls are typically (in fact, almost always) more effective than seller-to-executive calls. Utilize satisfied customers to contact potential clients as account sponsors to open the sales relationship.

Cold Calling

Asking for referrals and using executive networking principles are effective prospecting activities, but no prospecting game plan is complete without cold calling. Like the F-4 fighters being equipped with *only* bombs and missiles, they lacked a complete aerial arsenal without machine guns for close range fighting.

Although most salespeople recognize the need for cold calling, they don't like to make cold calls. In fact, only people who have it "floored in neutral" enjoy large doses of cold calling (They do exist; I've met them). Salespeople don't like making cold calls, and businesses don't like receiving cold calls, so why are people still cold calling? It's simple: it works. *Cold Calling is one of the most consistent lead generation methods in sales.* Regardless of who prospects (sales representatives, sales assistants, call centers, outsourcing centers, etc.), cold calling consistently generates more qualified leads and sets more appointments than any other prospecting method.

Cold calling is like the grit in the oyster that produces the pearl. It's estimated that every week close to one hundred million sales calls are made by telephone. Yearly these calls generate close to $380 billion dollars in sales revenue.

> **Note:** Because cold calling is a primary method for generating new opportunities, it is the principal focus of the remainder of this book.

Isaac Newton created a mathematically quantified account of gravitation that embraced terrestrial and celestial phenomena alike. In the process, he demolished the Aristotelian interpretation of the universe and established a physical basis for the Copernican universe. His laws, theories, and observations are regarded as scripture in the scientific community which still uses them today to guide spacecraft. When astronaut Bill Anders' son asked his father who was driving the Apollo 8 spacecraft, Anders replied, "I think Isaac Newton is doing most of the driving now."

By nature, Isaac Newton was a loner who did not revel in social settings. Filling his lonely days with books and research, Newton died a virgin. While a college student at Cambridge, he commented, "Plato is my friend, Aristotle is my friend, but my greatest friend is truth." Newton's constant quest for knowledge necessitated his inventing a new branch of mathematics titled calculus (an invention most college graduates wish he had not invented!). His search for knowledge was so extensive that he actually surpassed the existing theories and thoughts of his day.

Although it would be difficult to exaggerate Newton's contributions to science, he is most often remembered for his three laws of physics known as Newton's Laws.

Scholars and scientists who marvel at the inventions, discoveries, and creativity of Isaac Newton repeatedly ask, "What was his secret?" "How was he able to discover and accomplish so much?" "Was it really just pure intellectual genius?"

Newton's success was, of course, influenced by his rare intellectual genius. But his natural brilliance was not enough. Surviving drafts of Newton's primary work, *Principia*, support Thomas Edison's dictum that "Genius is 1 percent inspiration and 99 percent perspiration." Newton's work ethic and willingness to abandon previously held notions led to his unrivaled scientific discoveries. Newton was, in effect, "teachable" and ever ready to yield to new truths. This was particularly the case when the newly discovered truths flew in the face of assumed authority that was based on false conclusions. Newton tested everything. He did not merely rely on theory or assumptions.

———————

In like manner, successful prospecting is the result of hard work, persistence, and a willingness to test and implement intelligent prospecting strategies.

Total Market Opportunity

Isaac Newton's first law of motion states that mass persists in a state of rest unless acted upon by external forces. This scientific law is referred to as the principle of *inertia*. In sales, potential clients often remain in a state of inertia until acted upon by external forces that embrace effective prospecting skills and activities. In other words, most prospective clients remain in a state of complacency until nudged into action by sellers with the skills and strategies to generate interest.

In any given market, the majority of potential buyers are not actively looking for goods or services to purchase. Most markets reflect the 95 > 5 rule, which states that less than 5 percent of a total market opportunity is actively engaged in evaluating products or services. The remaining 95 percent is still a market opportunity but remains in a state of inertia unless advanced into a state of interest through effective prospecting.

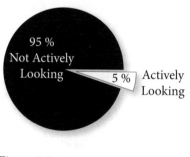

Figure 1.2

The purpose of prospecting is turning inactive opportunities into active opportunities. To achieve this objective, sellers need to implement prospecting skills that propel potential clients out of a state of inertia and into a state of interest.

CHAPTER 2

Overcoming Prospecting Fears

Our doubts are traitors
And make us lose the good we oft might win
By fearing to attempt.

—William Shakespeare

―――――◆―――――

In the winter of 1925, a deadly diphtheria epidemic broke out among the children of Nome, Alaska. Nome had no serum to combat the disease, and the nearest supply was 700 miles away in Anchorage. Given that the snow-covered landscape was virtually impassable, and the two state airplanes were in storage for the winter, the governor decided the serum would have to be "mushed" to Nome by a series of dogsled teams. After transporting the lifesaving serum to the town of Nenana by rail, officials delivered it to Wild Bill Shannon, whose dogsled team was the first of 18 teams to carry the serum 674 miles across the frozen tundra.

While the drivers raced against time, weather conditions could not have been worse as temperatures dipped to 40 degrees below zero, and gale-force winds created walls of blinding snow. On the fifth day, the sled carrying the serum lost all contact with the outside world, and Alaskans feared the worst. Suddenly, on the morning of February first—127 hours after the first dogsled team left Nenana—Gunnar Kaassen and his team of dogs emerged from the darkness, successfully delivering the serum to the children of Nome.

At times, conditions were so bad that Gunnar had to rely solely on his lead dog, Balto, for direction. Balto quickly became a celebrity throughout America when his picture was circulated by the press. He toured the country and even had a statue erected in his honor in New York's Central Park.

This epic journey of strength

and endurance is commemorated annually in the great Anchorage-to-Nome dogsled race named after the trail on which it is run: the Iditarod. Today, the Iditarod celebrates the men and dogs that conquered their fear of the brutal Alaskan winter and achieved one of the most heroic feats in U.S. history.

Conquering Our Fears

Like the dogsled teams in the race to Nome, salespeople who conquer their fears achieve seemingly impossible tasks, reach their goals, and accomplish their professional and financial objectives.

As sales managers, directors, and executives know, getting a team of sales professionals to spend 20 percent of its time prospecting can be incredibly challenging. As a former sales manager, I met regularly with our salespeople to discuss pipeline issues because many of them did not have a sufficient supply of qualified accounts. As we would discuss the need for cold calling, I noticed a clear and consistent pattern of explanations for avoiding cold calling. Explanation for avoiding cold calling was always emotional and never rational. I never had a salesperson say to me, "Patrick, cold calling is an absolute joke; only idiots cold call. No one here has ever closed a sale generated by a cold call!" It was impossible for them to make such a statement because the majority of our pipelines were built with cold calls, resulting in major sales.

I regularly train salespeople who tell me with great fervor that cold calling is a waste of time and that they have much more productive ways to generate leads. My standard response is, "Like what?" Typically, they respond with, "Well, for instance, contacting existing customers," "following up on current leads," or my personal favorite, "sending emails." I usually reply, "And how many qualified leads did you obtain last week from doing that?" The response is usually something like, "Well, I, uh,... ya,... uh... usually... let's see... uh, I think I got a couple of follow up emails." Right.

Explanations for not cold calling almost always migrate away from prospecting activities into other selling or marketing activities. One of these activities, for example, is following up on current leads, which is not a consistent method for generating new leads. Of course, if you call all of your existing leads and ask them for referrals that will be terrific. You will probably generate some excellent leads. It will also take you about an hour.

The pattern is always the same: sellers who avoid prospecting not only don't cold call, they don't engage in any regular lead generation activity. They wait around for leads to fall into their laps through advertising, Web sites, or client calls.

If you consistently fill your pipeline with qualified leads without cold calling, my hat is off to you. Close the book. It's been nice sharing time with you. On the other hand, if you are like the rest of the selling world, you could use more qualified leads and more appointments, and there is not a more consistent way to generate leads and set appointments than cold calling.

Three Reasons Sellers Avoid Cold Calling

I've often contemplated why so many salespeople dislike cold calling, and over time I've concluded that there is no single reason for it; however, consistent objections regularly surface. Based on research, interviews, and trainings, I have identified three common cold calling concerns which fall into the following three categories:

1. Cold calling can be uncomfortable: Many sellers find cold calling terribly unnatural. That's understandable. Most of us have been raised not to talk to strangers. Many sellers are uncomfortable with the "smile and dial" nature of cold calling. There is no doubt that "churn and burn" prospecting mentalities can be difficult to deal with.

2. Cold calling opens us up for rejection: Fear of rejection can be paralyzing. Most salespeople have a high need for acceptance. Because a large percentage of cold calls end in some form of refusal, just the thought of cold calling can make some people

physically ill. I had a workshop participant admit that he would rather be put into a potential buyer's voice mail than face a buyer verbally for fear of rejection.

3. Cold calling can be difficult: Many salespeople find cold calling to be the most trying aspect of selling. It takes mental discipline and emotional stamina to deal with the rejection that comes with cold calling. It takes self-control to set aside a certain amount of time each day to prospect. For many sellers, the discipline to cold call for an hour a day is a challenging habit to develop.

Challenge Brings Growth

Courage is resistance to fear, mastery of fear—not absence of fear.

—Mark Twain

Regardless of the challenges associated with cold calling, it is still one of the most productive prospecting activities in sales. Furthermore, every challenge provides an opportunity for growth as I learned in my senior year of high school.

My senior year of football taught me valuable lessons about overcoming challenges and endurance. Not only did we have a tough coach (a former lineman for the Los Angeles Rams), but he didn't like basketball players, and I was the starting point guard on the varsity basketball team. He thought basketball was a sport for wimps, (these were the days before Shaquille O'Neal and Karl Malone, when basketball was not yet a full-contact sport). Because I had spent the summer playing in basketball camps in Las Vegas and Los Angeles, I was unable to participate in the mandatory summer football weight lifting program. When I came back from basketball camp to start August two-a-day football practices, I was in for a shock. My coach informed me that because I had missed the summer weight lifting program, I was not eligible to start for the team. I was devastated, and to top it off, the coach informed me that the only way I could make up for the missed days was to lift weights for an hour each day at lunch between the morning and afternoon practices. Cramming weight lifting between two-a–days amounts to a nearly Herculean task, but I agreed to the schedule and for two weeks did three-a-days. Unbelievably challenging, it was the most difficult physical task I had ever faced. I threw up after sprints in evening practices. The spirit was willing, but the flesh was weak. I was so angry that I contemplated quitting.

Fortunately, I did not quit. In fact, I grew into such fantastic shape that by our first game I was in better physical condition than anyone on the team. I not only started at wing back on offense, I started at corner back on defense as well. I was our kick off and punt returner, and I went on to set a high school record for the most receptions in one game. (If it sounds like I'm bragging, I am. Oh, the glory days!)

More than simply creating a fond memory, my football experience taught me valuable lessons about life. I learned that by overcoming my weaknesses, I grow stronger. I also learned that behind every challenge there is an opportunity to mature and that any reward worth having is difficult to achieve. Most importantly, a hard day's labor with something to show for it feels great!

Cold calling is no different from the challenges I faced on that football team. When we face our challenges and conquer our fears, we accomplish great tasks.

Facing Prospecting Fears

Never take counsel from your fears.

—General George S. Patton

In order to overcome cold call reluctance, sellers need to face their fears head on. No one likes rejection or enjoys feeling uncomfortable. Difficult tasks can be daunting. Most human beings prefer the path of least resistance. Therefore, let me bluntly ask, "Why do it then? Is cold calling really worth it?" The answer is a resounding "Yes!" The reward is worth enduring the process. We may have our egos bruised along the way; in fact, we should expect it. By enduring this skin-thickening process, we reap experience, and we increasingly become proficient. This level of performance will give us the opportunity to look back and chuckle when we see the new guy desperately trying to disguise the fear-induced, eye-twitching, feeble attempts to justify not cold calling.

Over time, prospecting not only becomes easier, it becomes enjoyable. Successfully qualifying a lead or setting an appointment becomes one of the highs associated with selling.

When all is said and done, the key to eliminating cold calling anxiety is call volume. After making a few hundred cold calls, sellers lose their fear of cold calling. It really is that simple. The first few hundred calls are the toughest. Once sellers get past those initial calls, they typically lose cold call butterflies and realize that the outcome of a single call is not significant to their overall success.

The Point? It takes mental and emotional courage to conquer prospecting fears. Once conquered, however, sellers fill their calendars and pipelines with qualified leads and experience consistent selling success.

CHAPTER 3

Pipeline Management, Categories, and Terminology

———➤●◄———

While studying with Plato, Aristotle publicly disagreed with many of his teacher's ideas and philosophies. Consequently, Aristotle was banned from Plato's famed academy. Rather than being a setback, being banned from the academy liberated Aristotle from the abstract thinking of the school and allowed him to pursue his ideas in a manner unrestricted by the Socratic theory that non-physical forms such as truth and beauty were the keys to understanding. Aristotle maintained instead that sense, experience, and reason were the keys to understanding, and he developed methods of analysis and categorization that were based on observation and study.

Aristotle studied by dividing elements into constituent parts. Using a process of division, he set about categorizing the entire biological world. He grouped animals with similar characteristics into genera and then divided the genera into species. His chief grouping defined animals according to whether or not they had blood, which effectively divided them into groups known as vertebrates and invertebrates.

———➤●◄———

Aristotle's methods are still used by scientists today. In biology, plants and animals are classified by the structure of their bodies in a descending hierarchy of categories, a process called taxonomy: Kingdom, Phylum, Class, Order, Family, Genus, and Species. Remember your biology teacher reviewing the mnemonic saying, "King Phillip came over for good spaghetti?" Human beings, for example, progress through the following classification process:

- Kingdom: Animal
- Phylum: Chordates
- Class: Mammals
- Order: Primates
- Family: Hominidae
- Genus: Homo
- Species: Homo Sapiens

Scientists use the taxonomy system for clarity, organization, measuring purposes, and consistency.

The Science of Managing Sales Pipelines

Like the scientific process, effective sales processes use definitive categories to identify and track prospective clients. *The SONAR Selling System* uses a process similar to that of the taxonomy method in order to categorize and classify sales leads. Nine pipeline categories are used to track, manage, and report pipeline information (see *Figure* 3.1).

Pipeline categories are used to differentiate and represent the various stages buyers undergo before making a purchase. Sadly, what's not obvious to unsuccessful sellers is that not all leads are created equal. There is a difference, for example, between an unqualified lead and a qualified lead. There are even variations concerning qualified leads because some qualified leads are in the initial stages of the sales cycle, and some are "hot," ready to close.

Good pipeline management processes and programs differentiate and categorize the various stages buyers go through prior to making a purchase. These categories should be reflected in any type of lead tracking system—manual or electronic. Consistent pipeline terminology allows sales representatives, managers, and executives to manage with the force of facts using common contact management reports.[1]

---

1. In-depth pipeline analysis, reporting, forecasting, and management are integrated components of www.sonarcrm.com.

Sonar Pipeline Categories & Terminology[2]

Suspect — Targeted sales lead.

Dead — No longer a viable buyer

Qualified — Ultimate Decision Makers(s)
Available Funding
Acceptable Timeframe(s)
Matching Needs

Prospect — Qualified buyer who actively engages in the sales process.

Hold — Project timeframe delayed

Hot — Solution presentation delivered. Proposal sent. Decision date confirmed within specified timeframe.

Pending — Verbal or written commitment to purchase.

Lost — Chose a competitor

Won — Payment, purchase order, or contract received.

Figure 3.1

---

2. Some sales do not encompass the entire Sonar pipeline process. This process is a model, not a rigid formula. For less complex sales, or for sales with shorter sales cycles, categories can be modified and condensed to reflect market and industry specific sales cycles.

Manual Lead Tracking Systems

I am amazed at how hard people and organizations will work to obtain qualified leads; however, I am equally amazed at how easily they let qualified leads slip through their fingers. Call it apathy, lack of concentration, or just plain disorganization, but without proper pipeline management, leads, referrals, and potential clients fall between the cracks and are lost. As a result, business is lost.

There are multiple methods of tracking leads. You can use manual systems such as tickler files, appointment books, wall schedulers, calendars, notebooks, or index cards. In theory, these systems are simple and easy to use since you simply record relevant information about each lead on cards, paper, or calendars and then use them to follow up on sales leads. Sellers typically organize card systems by date of follow up so that they can look at any day of the month and know who to follow up with.

There is a downside to using a manual system; they are cumbersome. When pipelines grow, sellers end up with too many cards, pieces of paper and files. Things become confused, misplaced, and lost. Additionally, in most manual systems, information can only be retrieved by date of follow up, so if you need to look up a particular lead, you won't be able to locate it alphabetically. Manual systems also limit a seller's ability to create accurate pipeline and performance reports.

Electronic Contact Management Systems

Building and maintaining client relationships throughout the sales process requires accurate records of events, actions, comments, and expectations. Maintaining those records in a system that is easily accessible is critical to preserving long-term customer relations.

When communicating with buyers, or when prospects call back, sellers need to be able to quickly note conversations or access notes concerning previous conversations. Readily accessing information about past discussions demonstrates competence and gives customers added confidence that the seller is organized enough to manage their business.

Computers, software, PDA's, and the Internet provide sellers with lead tracking systems that are nothing short of fantastic. Sales automation and CRM (customer relationship management) programs such as ACT!, Goldmine, Sales Logix, Seibel Systems, SalesForce.com, SalesNet.com, SAP, and SonarCRM.com provide sellers with electronic lead tracking capabilities.

The beauty of using a software or Internet contact management program is that account data is cross-referenced so that it can be retrieved with the click of a mouse by name, location, date of follow-up, or sales category. You can print proposals, keep detailed notes, track an unlimited number of leads, and have multiple calendars without losing a thing. You can search by account name, callback date, location, or even by lead statuses like unqualified or qualified leads. The program even tells you who to call each day and includes detailed notes and information from previous discussions.

Salespeople reluctant to invest in modern technology need to ask themselves: "Is the *cost* of *not* having a modern lead tracking system more than the *price* of the software?"

> **Note:** Any salesperson serious about becoming a high-income earner has no option but to utilize modern technology. Technology gives sellers a competitive edge over salespeople who use manual pipeline management methods.

To find a lead tracking software program, sellers can search on the Internet under the titles "Contact Management," "Sales Automation," or, "Customer Relationship Management." You can also find contact management advertisements in sales and marketing publications such as *Power Selling* and *Sales and Marketing Management*.[3]

---

3. Visit www.sonarcrm.com to learn more about Patrick Henry & Associates sales force automation/CRM system.

SonarCRM

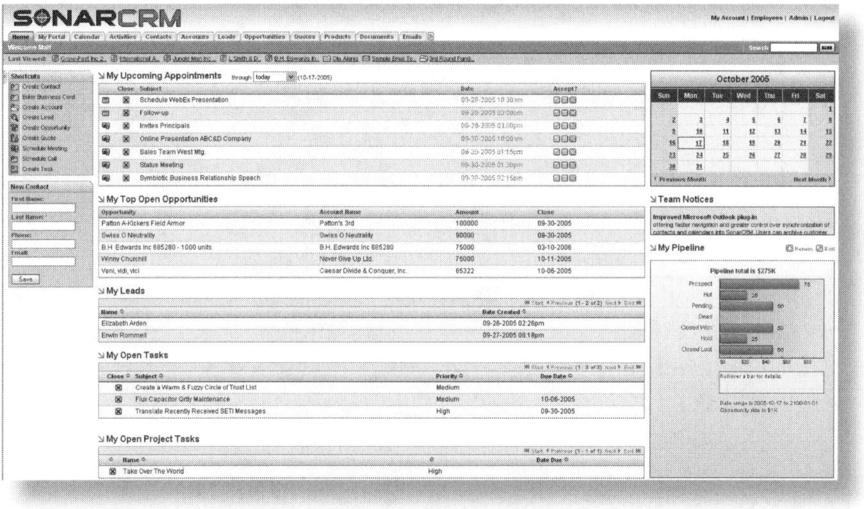

Figure 3.2

Internet based lead tracking systems such as *www.sonarcrm.com* allow sellers to manage pipelines remotely without having to load, upgrade, or maintain software. With access to the Internet, sellers can log in and retrieve pipeline data using ASP (application service provider) Internet programs. The programs are easy to learn, easy to use, and provide all of the capabilities necessary to easily track and manage leads. Furthermore, electronic lead tracking programs provide detailed reports that provide up-to-date information and reflect the overall health of a sales pipeline.

Although electronic contact management programs have pre-configured pipeline categories, terms, and definitions, most come equipped with the capability of adjusting the categories and terminology of the program to match the words, definitions, and language with which you are most comfortable.

Pipeline Reports for Sales Managers and Executives

———⇒●●⇐———

In 1814, Coalition forces from Prussia, Russia, Britain, and Sweden invaded France and marched on Paris. After twenty-one years of warfare, Napoleon Bonaparte was finally forced to abdicate and was exiled to the British controlled island of Elba. Astoundingly, in 1815 he was rescued from the island, resumed control of France and attacked the Coalition army in Belgium. On June 18th, the battle of Waterloo ensued when British commander Arthur Wellington counter attacked Napoleon. The fate of nations hung in the balance. If successful, Napoleon would bring another decade of war and conquest. If defeated, Europe could once again experience peace.

Perhaps no one had more riding on the battle than Nathan Rothschild. The London branch of the great Rothschild banking house had taken a keen interest in Wellington's attack. Nathan Rothschild had staked the family fortune on arming and supplying Wellington's vast army and had done so with British bonds.

Because the house of Rothschild was the largest single holder of British bonds, the outcome of the battle of Waterloo would forever alter its financial fate.

But Nathan Rothschild was no dummy. He and his family had developed a vast network of European informants and had created their own private messenger service. Day and night, the blue uniforms of the Rothschild couriers could be seen in coaches and in ships carrying messages, information, securities, notes, debts, and orders to buy or sell. Obviously, of all the information his agents delivered, the most urgent was the news they carried about battles, warfare, and weather—news that moved markets.

On the morning following Wellington's attack, the 19th of June, Nathan Rothschild slipped out of London and made his way to Folkestone Harbor to receive news from the other side of the English Channel. A few hours later, a Rothschild's agent arrived and handed him a *Dutch Gazette* newspaper with news of the battle. After scanning the headlines, he sped back to the London Exchange.

As he entered the Exchange, anticipation filled the room. The Rothschild reputation for inside information was well established and investors knew the stakes were high that day. Rothschild maintained a calm but stoic expression and then motioned to his brokers to begin selling his British bonds. This could only mean one thing: Wellington had been defeated. Panic struck the Exchange as Rothschild continued to sell, and sell, and sell more. Bond prices collapsed.

With the price of bonds almost completely worthless, Nathan suddenly reversed course and bought every British bond on the market—hundreds of thousands of pounds' worth of bonds. Moments later, and after he had cornered the entire British bond market, news of Napoleon's defeat by Wellington surfaced.

Because of the information network the Rothschilds had developed, in one day, and with one, bold stroke, the Rothschild family treasury was transformed into one of the world's largest fortunes ever known.

The Point? Information can pay big dividends. Sellers and managers who develop accurate information systems have a competitive edge over sellers and managers who don't.

Patrick Henry & Associates instructs sales managers and executives in *P⁴ Management Principles*—a management philosophy centered on the four elements of a successful sales organization: *People, Processes, Performance,* and *Profitability.* In order to implement *P⁴ Management Principles,* sales leaders must have consistent pipeline terminology and accurate reporting capabilities.

Pipeline classification and terminology are so vital that when *Patrick Henry & Associates* sets up *The SONAR Selling System* for sales teams, organizations, and businesses, one of our first goals is setting up or modifying contact management processes. We make this a high priority because without accurate pipeline classification, it's almost impossible to track, manage, report, or accurately forecast revenue projections.

Keeping track of potential clients and maintaining accurate pipeline categories takes organizational skill and discipline. Nevertheless, it is time well invested. Sales professionals and organizations that maintain accurate pipeline categories and terminology win more sales.

Sales managers and executives are tasked with making decisions that have enormous impact on sales organizations. Too often, sales leaders are not equipped with sufficient information to *manage with the force of facts*. They frequently make the mistake of basing decisions on gut feelings or emotions. Pipelines are often misunderstood and, as a result, forecasts are unreliable and inaccurate. Without available data and accurate reports, sales leaders rely on *guesswork* instead of *homework* to make decisions.

Several reports are critical to the success of sales organizations including:

1. Activity Reports
2. Pipeline Velocity Reports
3. Forecast Reports
4. Win/Loss Reports
5. Account Briefing Reports (For complex sales)

The two most essential reports for measuring and maintaining healthy pipelines are *Pipeline Velocity Reports* and, for complex, committee-based sales, *Account Briefing Reports*.

Pipeline Velocity Reports

SONARCRM.com provides *Pipeline Velocity Reports* that track the overall health, value, and progression of sales pipelines. Using data from *SONARCRM.com* (or other reputable sales automation and CRM programs), we create customized reports that trace the time it takes to

Sample SonarCRM Pipeline Velocity Reports

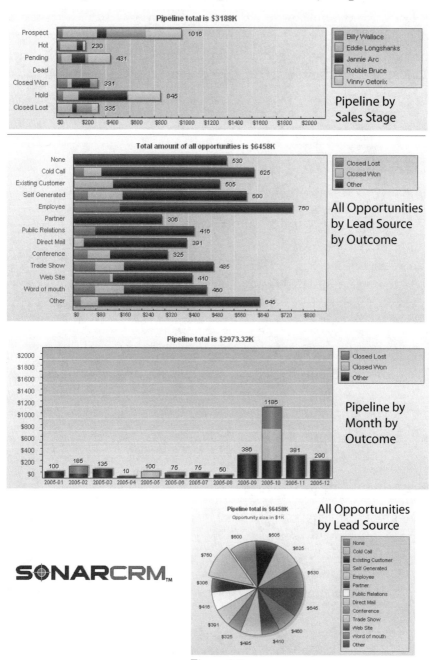

Figure 3.3

progress prospects from one pipeline category to the next, i.e., the velocity. For example, by using *Pipeline Velocity Reports*, a manager can determine the exact number of qualified accounts, hot prospects, and pending sales in an individual or overall pipeline *and* track the exact activity and progression of those accounts on a weekly, monthly, or quarterly basis.[4]

Pipeline Velocity Reports provide sales representatives, managers, and executives with the following capabilities:

- Determining *exact* sales cycles (no more guessing)
- Measuring *actual* individual and team performance
- Managing and coaching with *factual* pipeline data
- Identifying *precise* pipeline strengths and vulnerabilities
- Establishing *realistic* prospecting goals and standards
- Identifying *specific* individual and team skill deficiencies (prospecting, investigating, presenting, closing, etc.)
- Establishing fair and *practical* territory sizes and boundaries
- Determining *percentages* of change (velocity) between categories
- Creating *accurate* sales forecasts and revenue projections

Armed with pipeline velocity data, sales managers and executives measure the progression and value of a pipeline, manage performance on an individual and team basis, and create consistent, accurate revenue projections.

Account Briefing Reports

Account briefing reports are used to manage complex, committee-based sales that involve high-dollar products and multiple decision makers. Account briefing reports help sellers and managers work collaboratively to analyze high-dollar accounts and develop corresponding selling, presenting, and competitive strategies.

---

4. To learn how *Pipeline Velocity Reports* can help your business or sales organization, contact *Patrick Henry & Associates, Inc.* at 1 (877) 204-4341.

Sample SONAR Account Briefing Report

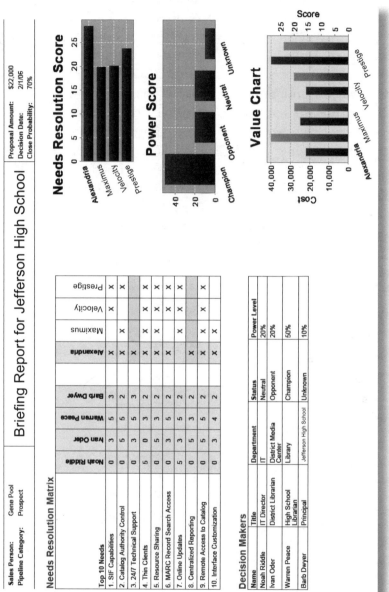

Figure 3.4

To manage complex, committee-based sales, *SonarCRM.com* provides an electronic opportunity management module called SONAR (Strategize, Organize, Navigate & Respond). In addition to sales force automation and CRM services, SONAR facilitates information gathering and evaluation that is essential to winning complex sales. SONAR transforms acquired data into a comprehensive briefing report that calculates critical decision factors including: needs resolution in comparison to competitors, decision making power by title or department, value charts that measure needs resolution in comparison to competing pricing, available communication channels, qualification logistics, and related data necessary to evaluate large accounts, identify strengths and weaknesses, and overcome potential vulnerabilities.[5]

SONAR briefing reports simplify complex sales by identifying:

- The top ten critical needs of the account
- Departments involved in the sale
- Competitors involved in the sale
- Analysis of fulfillment of the top ten needs in comparison to competitors
- Top decision makers by department and order of decision-making power
- Funding, qualification, and decision process logistics
- Competitive analysis and SWOT (Strengths, Weaknesses, Opportunities, Threats) data

Using SONAR, sales and marketing teams work collaboratively to design competitive strategies, develop tactical presentation content, "response block" product deficiencies, construct overall account stratagems, and effectively plan, forecast, and close complex sales.

---

5. For more information regarding SONAR, contact *Patrick Henry & Associates, Inc.* at 1 (877) 204-4341 or visit or www.sonarsales.com.

In Summary

Successfully managing sales leads, relationships, and processes means that sales individuals and organizations must use consistent pipeline terminology, a common sales language, and a reputable sales automation or CRM program.

Highly successful sales managers and executives build effective organizational models and reporting systems. With modern phone systems, CRM programs, accurate pipeline data, and SONAR briefing reports, sales organizations retrieve the necessary information for creating accurate reports, making intelligent decisions, and winning more sales.

CHAPTER 4

Defining Your Target Market

Better to return and make a net, than to go down to the stream and merely wish for fish.

—Chinese Proverb

The Bay of Pigs fiasco in 1961 is a classic example of not having a clear and definitive objective when taking action. Tired of the growing threats of Fidel Castro and his communist acolytes, President John Kennedy agreed to support an invasion of Cuba by anti-Castro Cuban exiles. Kennedy initially agreed to provide American forces to support the exiled Cubans' attempt to overthrow Castro and install a democratic government. Regrettably, like many well-intentioned politicians, Kennedy allowed his fear of international censure to sway his better judgment, and at the last minute, withdrew U.S. forces from the invasion. The President's last minute removal of naval and air support left the Cuban exiles abandoned on a beachfront to face Castro's troops alone. Outnumbered, outgunned, and betrayed. Castro made quick work of the freedom fighters at a tropical bay now known infamously as The Bay of Pigs. Every anti-Castro freedom fighter was either killed or taken captive.

Kennedy's political calculations undermined his objective to rid the world of a dictator, Fidel Castro, and led to an episode that embarrassed not only his administration, but also his country.

Identifying Prospecting Objectives

President Kennedy's blunder at The Bay of Pigs illustrates the importance of having a clearly defined objective and taking decisive steps to achieve that objective.

Repeatedly, I encounter sellers prospecting without first identifying and defining their target market. Without any pre-account planning or preparation, many sellers just pick up the phone and start "dialing for dollars."

There are sellers who have concluded that cold calling doesn't work. In fairness, this is a correct conclusion when it is done the wrong way. Doing it the wrong way will simply reinforce the pre-conceived notion that it is a waste of time. It must be done correctly.

I cannot over-emphasize the importance of defining a target market because *sellers who don't take the time to clearly identify their target market prior to cold calling waste time, money, and effort on leads who will never purchase.* Without a well-defined market, salespeople invest time cold calling with only diminishing returns, and severely limit their opportunities for success. **The key to being successful is finding a target-rich environment.**

> **Caution!** Poorly defined markets are like poorly defined targets. If you don't know what you are shooting at, chances are you won't hit it.

To conduct a successful teleprospecting campaign, a seller should first define his or her target market by differentiating high probability buyers from low probability buyers. High probability buyers meet certain criteria that make them likely to purchase your goods or services. In other words, they have certain credentials and characteristics that make them probable buyers: whereas, low probability buyers do not have characteristics that make them likely to buy.

High Probability Buyers

High probability buyers are potential customers who match *optimum* demographic and geographic qualifications. In other words, they are the *most* likely accounts to purchase your products or services. High probability buyers maximize return on investment for the TIME (Time, Investment, Money & Effort) spent cold calling. They have certain characteristics that lead you to believe they both need your product or service, and have the ability to buy it.

Low Probability Buyers

Low probability buyers are potential customers who match *minimum* demographic and geographic qualifications. In other words, they are the *least* likely accounts to purchase your products or services. Low probability buyers minimize return on investment for the TIME (Time, Investment, Money & Effort) spent cold calling. They could potentially become customers, but they do not have the characteristics that lead you to believe they are an ideal fit for your good or service. Not big enough, not wealthy enough, wrong location, not enough employees, etc., are potential examples of reasons particular accounts would be low probability buyers.

By identifying and distinguishing high probability buyers from low probability buyers, sellers avoid making the beginner mistake of spending time searching for prospects who cannot or will not purchase.

> **The Point?** Power prospecting is based on the premise that quality calls are preferred to quantity calls. Effective cold calling strategies focus on preliminarily qualifying contact lists and identifying high probability buyers—*prior to cold calling.*

Demographics

There are two factors that are traditionally used to define a target market: demographics and geographics.

Since you want to identify the market that is going to give you the largest return on investment (ROI), the first step is matching favorable demographics with product or service capabilities. Cerebral sellers calculate return on investment by dividing the profitable dollar amount of the sale by the amount of time invested to get it.

$$\frac{\text{Profitable \$ Amount}}{\text{Invested Sales Time}} = \text{ROI}$$

To maximize return on investment, sellers should prioritize each prospecting moment spent with high probability buyers and invest the majority of their efforts with the candidates who have the greatest purchasing capability. "Cherry picking" is smart business, and there's nothing wrong with it. Sharp business people go after low hanging fruit by matching demographics to prospects who will most likely need the offered goods or services and who have the ability to buy it.

Demographics: The characteristics of human populations and population segments, especially when used to identify consumer markets. (*The American Heritage Dictionary*, 3rd Edition).

Good sellers identify markets that have the demographic numbers that match their capabilities. For example, if you are selling roping equipment to western tack stores, you probably don't need to worry yourself to death if your potential stores are not Fortune 500 companies. If, on the other hand, you are selling million dollar oil drilling equipment, you will want to focus your energies on prospects that are at least Fortune 1000 companies.

The most frequently used business-to-business sales demographics are:

1. Gross sales (for example, $25 million)
2. Number of employees (for example, 75)
3. Number of years in business (for example, 5)
4. Company ranking (for example, one of the top 100 fastest growing businesses in Texas. A Fortune 500, 1000, etc.)

For business-to-consumer sales such as life insurance agents, real estate agents, and bank loan officers, you should, obviously, establish a target market based on demographics specific to your industry. Examples of business-to-consumer demographics might include:

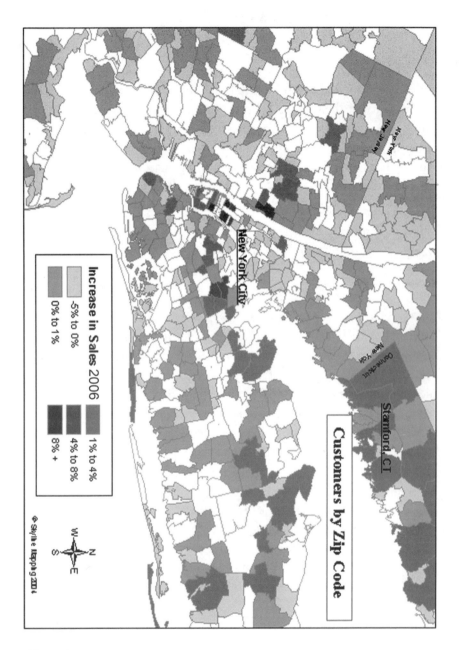

Figure 4.1

1. Household income
2. Personal gross income
3. Age
4. Sex
5. Married or single
6. Credit rating

It is critical to narrow the definition of your target market from broad classifications to specific definitions. For instance, you should fine-tune a statement such as "All companies that could use our product or service" to "All companies with more than 100 employees that could use our goods or services," or "all companies that generate more than $5 million in gross sales," etc.

In a major metropolitan area, I once purchased a chamber of commerce directory in order to sell sales training. As our team began calling, our "hit" ratio was unbelievably low. After hearing "not interested" a few hundred times, we decided to bag the list because it was just too broad. I called a technology association located in the same city and purchased their directory. We went through the list and identified the exact demographics we were looking for: companies grossing a minimum of two million in sales and operating a sales force of at least five representatives. After our analysis of our new demographic standards, our cold call hit ratio quadrupled based on the changes we made.

Large businesses or companies with sufficient funding will find it worthwhile to hire professional demographic research specialists who use hard data to identify specific market niches. Professional Geographic Information System (GIS) services locate demographics that match exact market specifications and create sales maps, potential client maps, customer maps, and demographic data lists. Such professionals determine buying patterns by county, voting district, zip code, or other geographic parameters and create a profile for your business to target which consists of existing ideal customers, vendors, or distributor demographics applied to other counties, voting districts, or zip codes that share the same demographics. These services provide businesses with the maximum ammunition to penetrate their target markets.[1]

Geographics

Geographics deal with locations such as zip code, city, county, state, territory, province, or country. For example, in most industries you should probably avoid cold calling Bangladesh. If you are a traveling life insurance agent, you don't want to cold call areas more than 100 miles away. If you are selling long distance services that cater to metropolitan needs, you want to find geographic locations that match your capabilities and product focus.

Geographic data can also be used for "blitzkrieg" tactics when a seller targets a specific sales territory. Territories comprised of a high density of existing customers are easily identifiable with geographic data. Once identified, specific sales strategies can be implemented to exploit a large referral base in a geographic area. "Beachfront" techniques can be used to blanket areas that have large numbers of potential or existing clients.

Target Market Chart

Demographics	Geographics
1.	1.
2.	2.
3.	3.
4.	4.

Figure 4.2

---

1. For more information on GIS (Geographic Information System) services, or to view sample maps, visit www.PatrickHenryInc.com and click on the *Skyline Mapping* icon.

> **The Point?** Use demographic and geographic data to preliminarily qualify potential cold calling lists and fine-tune prospecting strategies.

Target Markets

I am currently on the board of directors of a nutritional supplement company in Salt Lake City, Utah—the Mecca of the nutritional industry. I was initially involved in their business as a sales consultant at a time when they were scrambling to get their supplements into health food stores and fitness centers. They had established thriving businesses in Japan and Thailand but could not seem to gain a permanent foothold in the United States. Upon researching their market, competitors, and existing clients, I discovered that their definition of a target market was too broad. They were using contact lists that included anyone and everyone involved in the nutritional industry.

As I scrutinized the data they were using to target accounts, it became apparent that a large percentage of their leads were multi-level marketers, many of whom were individuals selling a single line of products out of their garages or home offices. These individuals were not their appropriate target market. Another large percentage of their leads were the hundreds of GNC stores seen in every mall across America; however, because most GNC store decisions are made at the corporate level, it was a waste of time to call each store individually.

In addition to dietary products, this company also provided on-site nutritional analysis services. For that reason we decided to initially target accounts that were easily accessible from Salt Lake City: midwestern and western states. Once we established a strong presence in the west, we then directed the business eastward.

When we initiated our prospecting program, we narrowed our target market to the following demographic and geographic parameters. Targeted accounts had to meet these criteria:

1. Have been in business at least one year (stability, established clientele, etc.)

2. Be located west of the Mississippi River
3. Have a "brick and mortar" retail store (versus a home-based business)
4. Be locally owned and operated (non-chain stores)

We established a call center to cold call each of our targeted accounts and the results were phenomenal. Sales skyrocketed. Once we restricted our efforts to high probability, strategically profiled accounts, sales increased so exponentially that the company could barely keep up with shipping and manufacturing demands—a problem they were happy to deal with.

Ideal Customer Profiles

Good salespeople narrow their target market by identifying ideal customers. Information about existing clients is a literal goldmine of usable data.

Customer profiles typically include business size, number of employees, gross sales, business type, products or services purchased, location, and other account specific data.

To identify your ideal customers use the *Ideal Customer Profile Chart*.

Ideal Customer Profile Chart

Best Customers	Characteristics	Worst Customers	Characteristics
1.		1.	
2.		2.	
3.		3.	
4.		4.	
5.		5	

Figure 4.3

In the first column (from left to right) list a minimum of five of your best customers. *Your best customers are those clients who give you the maximum amount of profit with the fewest number of problems.* Start with your favorite customers, the accounts that make you grin every time you hear their names, placing your absolute best customer as number one and listing your second best customer next and so on.

Next to the best customers bracket is a column called the characteristics column. This column helps you identify *why* the accounts you selected are ideal. To identify ideal customer characteristics ask yourself, "Why are they the best?" After completing your list of positive characteristics, analyze and then list what common attributes your best clients exemplify.

The next bracket is the worst customers column. You should follow the same pattern and identify your worst customers: *those clients who give you the greatest number of problems with the least amount of profit,* the customers who make you cringe every time you hear their names. Starting with your least favorite customer, put that customer as number one, and then list your second worst customer and so on.

Adjacent to the worst customers column is another characteristics column. This column helps identify consistent characteristics of problem accounts. In the same manner as the best customer characteristics, you must ask yourself, "Why are they the worst customers?" You should analyze and then list the negative characteristics of these customers. The data you gather from this process should be used to recognize consistent traits or patterns with problem accounts that can be used to avoid these types of accounts in the future.

Once you have identified your best and worst clients and their associated characteristics, you are able to determine who your ideal customer is, thereby narrowing your target market to match the characteristics of your ideal and most profitable customers.

Information Lists

In order to establish intelligent prospecting strategies, sellers need to use professional information lists that provide both demographic and geographic data, preferably in an electronic format. Electronic information lists can be rented, purchased, or even borrowed, and in most cases, they can be imported into contact management programs or into Excel spreadsheets for clarity, notes, and reporting purposes.

Three primary sources of information lists are available that are used to identify target markets:

1. Purchased information lists
2. Free information lists
3. Internet search directories

Purchased Information Lists

Reliable sources for purchased information lists include Dun & Bradstreet, Hoover's, InfoUSA, A.C. Nielsen, list brokers, and trade publications that sell customer subscription lists. If you need list brokers, you can find them in your local Yellow Pages under "Mailing Lists," "Direct Mail," or "Mailing List Brokers." Direct-marketing publications such as *Direct Marketing* or *Target Marketing* carry "Mailing List" ads that list catalogs available for rent or purchase. There is even a free catalog, put out by Edith Roman Associates in New York City, which you can use to identify an information list that meets your target market.

Information lists range in cost between 5 and 25 cents per name, depending on the amount of data you are seeking. Depending on the quality and specifications of the information list, contact names can cost as much as $10 a name.

I highly recommend that you purchase information lists. Purchased lists are usually more accurate, up-to-date, and are available in multiple electronic formats. Typically, the more expensive the list the more accurate the data.

When you purchase information lists, be sure to investigate the quality of the data prior to making the purchase by asking the list vendor the following questions:

✓ How accurate is the list? (Accuracy is everything. Time,

energy, and money will be wasted if the list contains inaccurate information).

✓ When was the last time the list was updated?

✓ How is the list organized?

✓ What electronic formats are available?

✓ Do you have references that I can contact to ask list quality related questions?

Purchasing your information lists from reputable sources will increase your ROI (return on investment) and ensure that you avoid wasting time on faulty or inaccurate data.

> **Note:** You can significantly increase your cold call response rate if you start your calls at the end of the list and work backwards. Everyone calls AAA Widgets, but how often does Zygot International get called?

Free Information Lists

The second source for prospecting names are free lists that are available from organizations such as state and community government agencies, public libraries, some chambers of commerce, and various online lists found on the Internet. Some sellers don't realize, however, that the best and most accurate free information list is a standard telephone directory.

Although these free lists are ideal for start up businesses that sell community oriented goods and services, they are not ideal for general prospecting purposes. Excluding telephone directories, their data is normally not as accurate, up-to-date, or complete as purchased information lists, which means your time will be wasted sifting through cluttered data, calling accounts with disconnected numbers, and spending time on calls that won't purchase.

Internet Search Directories

The third source for prospecting lists is Internet search directories such as *www.Switchboard.com, www.YellowPages*.com, and other web sites that offer directory searches. Most major search engines, such as *www. Google.com*, have directory search capabilities where sellers are able to identify businesses by description and location. For example, if you are selling pharmaceutical drugs to pharmacies in Atlanta, type in "pharmacies" and list "Atlanta" as the point of inquiry for your search, and you will get a results page that lists pharmacy stores in Atlanta. You can then copy and paste or type the directory information into an Excel spreadsheet or contact management program.

In Summary

In order to maximize prospecting efforts, sellers must first identify their target market and then obtain organized and accurate lists to contact that market. Armed with a list of high probability buyers, sellers ensure their return on investment is high. Without quality information lists, sellers waste time finding names, locating numbers, looking up business addresses, and fumbling through data. Without organized lists of potential buyers, sellers stay busy, but they don't set appointments or qualify accounts.

> **The Point?** Successful sellers focus on speaking to the right people. Increase "hit ratios" and maximize your return on investment by strategically narrowing and defining your target market.

CHAPTER 5

Developing Your Unique Selling Proposition

People don't buy Disneyland tickets, they buy fun.

—Anonymous

———◦———

In 1487, Christopher Columbus managed to arrange a meeting with the monarchs of Spain—King Ferdinand and Queen Isabella. Columbus had spent years searching for financiers for his proposed voyage to discover a shorter route to Asia. He originally approached the Italian and Portuguese aristocracy for support, but to no avail. Eventually he finagled a meeting with the king of Portugal, John II. In his meeting with King John, he detailed his plans for the voyage and the necessary funding and equipment needed to accomplish his expedition. In return for financing the voyage, Columbus made serious demands on the king, including the title of Grand Admiral of the Oceanic Seas, the office of viceroy over the lands he discovered, and 10 percent of the future commerce with such lands.

After King John II declined his offer, Columbus decided to change his approach. Rather than talk about the details of the proposed voyage, he would focus exclusively on the financial benefits to the financiers, and the public glory associated with navigational discoveries. He decided to center his discussions on the interests of his audience—their greed, desire for fame, or need for wealth. His strategy worked magnificently.

Although Columbus was an unproven explorer, and knew less about oceanic navigation than the average sailor, in one area he was an absolute genius. Christopher Columbus knew how to persuade an audience. He had developed an amazing power to charm and convince his listeners by focusing on their vanity, conceit, and self-interest—and not his own. Queen Isabella was no exception. Columbus spent years in the queen's court convincing her of the financial and geopolitical benefits of establishing a shorter trade route to Asia. His strategy finally paid off. With the Spanish defeat of the Moorish invaders in 1492, and the wartime burden of the treasury lifted, King Ferdinand and Queen Isabella decided to patronize Columbus' maritime expedition. On August 3rd, 1492, Columbus set sail with three ships, equipment, the salary of the sailors, and a lucrative contract for himself. Although his mission failed to discover a shorter trade route to Asia, he made the most influential exploratory discovery of all time—the Americas.

Had Christopher Columbus continued making presentations focused on the details of the exploration instead of the financial benefits associated with funding the exploration, he probably would never have made his famous journey.

Columbus, however, was cerebral. He adjusted his approach and focused on the benefits the financiers would experience with the success of the proposed voyage rather than the features of the voyage itself.

Focus on Benefits

Every experienced salesperson has been advised to "Focus on benefits, not features." Nevertheless, how many salespeople actually know how to distinguish features from benefits? More importantly, how many of them implement the advice? Most salespeople repeatedly violate this principle, not because they disagree with the advice, but because they do not know *how* to implement it.

To avoid delivering a "feature bomb," sellers need to resist the natural instinct to jump in and tell buyers all about their good or service. For example, let's say a buyer shows an interest in a product by asking, "Does your air filtering system eliminate odors?" Non-cerebral salespeople immediately respond by providing a laundry list of capabilities. "Why of course. Our air filtering system not only eliminates odor, it also eradicates dust, fungus, and helps people with allergies breathe better. Not only that, this particular air filter..." Cerebral sellers, on the other hand, avoid delivering "data dumps" and instead question buyer inquiries. "Are you currently experiencing odor problems?" "How bad is it?" "What do you think might be the cause of the odor?" Rather than spewing a list of features, intelligent sellers identify the exact needs, concerns, and motives of buyers, and then address them.

A colleague asked me to assist him negotiate the purchase of a new truck. As he was examining a particular model, a salesperson approached him and said, "This truck has special equipment designed for pulling boats and trailers." My colleague responded, "I don't have a boat or a trailer, and I don't want to pay extra for features I won't use." By immediately hammering on the features of the truck, this salesperson actually deterred my colleague from buying.

I listened to a salesperson carry on and on about the capability of his customer service staff to support its clients in eleven languages. The buyer responded, "That's nice, but we only operate in the U.S. and don't need that."

There are multiple steps salespeople should follow in order to drive home the benefits of their products and solutions rather than the features. The first step is identifying the needs, pains, and problems that buyers experience. The second step is using the *Needs-Resolution Matrix* (see *Figure* 5.1) to differentiate product features, advantages, and benefits—and then matching them to product solutions. The third step is using solution-benefit questions to help buyers see the benefits of implementing proposed solutions.

Using *SONAR's Needs-Resolution Matrix* to Develop a Unique Selling Proposition

Rather than focusing on benefits and solutions, many salespeople engage in low level feature wars that distract buyers from grasping the benefits of proposed solutions. More often than not, salespeople just feature buyers to death. This is especially true with cold calls. Sellers often "throw out" features hoping a few might stick.

Doing a little homework and identifying potential benefits prior to cold calling can make a huge difference. Successful prospectors identify a target rich environment and develop a USP based on value creation. The way to craft a message based on value creation is to focus on client needs and problems.

After a tour of duty overseas, a certain officer was appointed to a stateside induction center where he advised new recruits regarding their government benefits, specifically G.I. insurance. Within a few months, he had an almost one hundred percent sales record.

His supervisors were amazed at his extraordinary achievement. Rather than ask him how he accomplished such a remarkable rate of success, one of his superiors stood in the back of the room while the officer delivered his presentation. The officer introduced the general provisions of the G.I. insurance to the new recruit. He then concluded his presentation by saying, "If you buy G.I. insurance, go into battle and are killed, the government will have to pay $35,000 to your beneficiaries. If you don't buy G.I. insurance, go into battle and are killed, the government will only have to pay a maximum of $3,000. Now, which group of soldiers do you think will be sent into battle first?

Note: People don't buy features. They buy benefits. They buy solutions to problems. The world's best product or service is worthless if it fails to solve a problem or satisfy a buyer's needs.

The key to focusing on benefits instead of features is to distinguish product benefits and features prior to cold calling. The best way you can ensure that a cold call focuses on benefits is to clearly identify the benefits a product or service provides prior to cold calling.

Differentiating benefits and features is not always as easy as it sounds. In order to assist salespeople in making the distinction, I recommend using *SONAR's Needs-Resolution Matrix*. *The Needs-Resolution Matrix* is a sales, marketing, and presentation tool designed to analyze products and services in problem-solving terms. It was created to assist sales and marketing professionals when they need to identify and understand the differences between buyer pains and problems, product features, advantages, and benefits.

The key to using *The Needs-Resolution Matrix* is focusing on client pains and problems first, addressing products, features, and advantages second. For example, list every possible problem and pain experienced by potential clients before analyzing the best solution to address those pains and problems.[1]

The Needs-Resolution Matrix

Category	Need-Problem	Pain	Solution	Benefit
The category of analysis: industry, market, business, department, end-user, etc.	A need, dissatisfaction, difficulty, or problem.	The result or consequence of unfulfilled needs &/or unresolved problems.	Product features & capabilities that address needs, problems, & pains.	The result of fulfilled needs, resolved problems & eliminated pain.
Department: Quality Control	*Updating Manufacturing safety documents*	*Failed FDA audit*	*Maximus Version 4.0*	*No more failed FDA audits due to poor safety document updates.*

Figure 5.1

There are five steps used in *The Needs-Resolution Matrix*:

1. Identify the *category* of analysis (industry, market, business, department, person, job title, etc.).

2. Identify the *needs* and/or *problems* experienced by the category selection.

3. Identify the *pains* experienced by the category selection, i.e., the consequences of unfulfilled needs or unresolved problems.

---

1. *The Needs-Resolution Matrix* is an integrated componenet of SONAR. Visit www.sonarsales.com to view an electronic version of *The Needs-Resolution Matrix.*

SONAR's Needs-Resolution Matrix

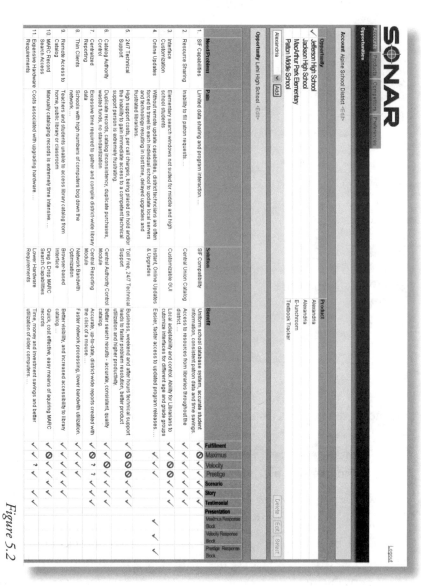

Figure 5.2

4. Identify the *solution* that resolves the buyer's pain.

5. Identify the *benefits* to the buyer of fulfilling the need, resolving the problem, and eliminating the pain.

Once you have identified client pains and problems, and the product features and advantages to resolve those pains and problems, you are prepared to create a winning cold call script by incorporating the identified benefits into the presentation.

> **Note:** Benefits only apply to explicit needs. You may have some nifty features, but if product capabilities don't address specific client pains and problems, they are advantages, not benefits.

Information gathered from *The Needs-Resolution Matrix* equips salespeople with the information needed to shift from the general to the specific. Salespeople can take the general needs and pains of prospects and apply them to the specific capabilities and solutions of their products. Using this information, salespeople can adapt the presentation to cover selected features that offer advantages relevant to the prospect's criteria, i.e., the benefits of the product or service. By keeping track of the needs and problems of buyers and then creating scripts and presentations to address and solve those needs and problems, sellers ensure that they focus their presentation efforts on the benefits of their solution.

Because product features are meaningless unless they help buyers eliminate pains and problems, winning salespeople use *The Needs-Resolution Matrix* to demonstrate how their proposed products and features can fulfill needs, eliminate problems, and reduce pain—in other words, the benefits of the proposed product or service.

Solution-Benefit Questions

(Review *The DNASelling Method* in chapter 11). The DNASelling Method consists of:

Discovery-Qualification Questions: Questions that discover a buyer's existing circumstance, account facts, qualification factors, and purchasing capabilities.

Need-Problem Questions: Questions that identify a buyer's needs, problems, and primary buying motives.

Ascertain-Pain Questions: Questions that ascertain the negative consequences of unfulfilled needs and/or unresolved problems, i.e., the pain.

Solution-Benefit Questions: Questions that focus on the benefits of need and problem resolution.

The final step of *The DNASelling Method* is asking solution-benefit questions. Solution-benefit questions focus on the value of solving problems and resolving pains. They center on the benefits of the presented solution. They move prospects from recognizing the impact of the current problems to focusing on the benefits of the recommended solution. *In other words, solution-benefit questions emphasize the positive benefits of solving identified problems.*

Sales professionals are often labeled and stereotyped as clones with habitual and predictable behavioral patterns. Unfortunately, the same can be said of buyers. Far too often, prospects focus on the minute details of product or service capabilities and fail to recognize or see the "big picture." It is a salesperson's job to move buyers away from understanding functional capabilities to understanding explicit product or service benefits. Sellers need to help prospects catch the vision of the product or service's benefits by asking solution-benefit questions.

The primary advantage of asking solution-benefit questions is getting prospects to verbalize product benefits. For instance, if a salesperson asks a buyer, "How would a faster network increase the productivity of your technical staff?" A buyer might respond, "It would definitely speed up the process of transferring large data files across our network." Solution-benefit questions get buyers to articulate the benefits of problem resolution and, in turn, convince themselves of the value of the solution.

Men are best convinced by reasons that they themselves discover.

—Benjamin Franklin

Although solution-benefit questions are primarily used during the investigation portion of the sales cycle, they can also be asked during the presenting and closing stage of the sales cycle. Many sellers ask solution-benefit questions during sales presentations to summarize topics, points, or benefits. They also ask the questions again at the conclusion of the presentation in order to sum up the benefits of the product or solution.

Sample *Solution-Benefit* Questions

After helping buyers ascertain the pain associated with an identified problem, cerebral sellers turn their attention to the benefits of implementing the solution by asking solution-benefit questions.[2]

- How valuable would it be for you to be able to _____?
- What benefits do you see from resolving [X issue]?
- Suppose you could eliminate _____, how beneficial would that be?
- How might this feature benefit you?
- Suppose you could _____, how would that help you?
- How will improving _____ affect your organization?
- What do you see as the benefits of this approach?
- What benefits do you see from implementing X capability?
- How would _____ improve _____?

---

2. See Chapter 8 in *The DNASelling Method* to learn how to ask effective Ascertain-Pain and Solution-Benefit questions.

- Is there any other way _____could help you?
- Is there any other way that _____ could help?

Because good questions don't just roll off the top of a salesperson's head, it is important to develop solution-benefit questions prior to presenting. An excellent way to create solution-benefit questions is to identify ways in which your product or service benefits buyers. You can then convert those benefits into questions.

> **Note:** Amateur salespeople sell products. Cerebral sales professionals sell solutions. Use the above questions to focus on benefits, solutions, and positive consequences associated with problem resolution.

Benefit Validation Statements

In addition to using solution-benefit questions, another useful, yet simple tactic for focusing on benefits and not features is using benefit validation statements. Benefit validation statements are short sentences that boldly state the benefits associated with product or service capabilities. Example benefit validation statements include:

The benefit of X capability to you is _____.

What this means to you is _____.

The benefit of implementing ABC product is _____.

Benefit validation statements help salespeople communicate and emphasize the benefits linked to product features and capabilities. They are also excellent tools for summarizing benefits.

Features: Don't Throw the Baby out with the Bath Water!

By emphasizing the importance of focusing on benefits, I am not implying that salespeople should leave out any mention of the product features and capabilities that create the benefits. On the contrary, features form an important part of the sales process. Features must be demonstrated, but only in order to focus on the benefits the buyer gains from using the product. Don't throw the baby out with the bathwater. Discuss and demonstrate features to introduce and validate the linked benefit.

In Summary

For ultimate impact, salespeople should address the needs, goals, and objectives of buyers and focus on the benefits buyers will experience by implementing your product or service.

Using *The Needs-Resolution Matrix*, salespeople can clearly distinguish benefits from features. By asking solution-benefit questions, salespeople help buyers articulate and verbalize product solutions. By selling solutions, salespeople demonstrate the benefits associated with their product or service.

> **The Point?** Remember: Disneyland doesn't sell rides—they sell fun. Black and Decker doesn't sell drills—they sell holes. Orthodontists don't sell braces—they sell smiles. People buy benefits, not features. Sell benefits.

Use *The Needs Resolution Matrix* to develop scripts, questions and unique propositions that focus on product or service benefits and not features.[3]

---

3. Visit www.sonarsales.com to view an electronic version of *The Needs-Resolution Matrix*.

CHAPTER 6

Qualification vs. Appointment-based Cold Calls

———◦◦◦———

Marcius Porcius (Cato) was a Roman statesman born at Tuscalum in 234 B.C. Living up to his surname, which signified "the wise," Cato became a distinguished leader in Roman politics, and was sent to Carthage in 175 B.C. to make a treaty between the Numidians and Carthaginians. It was during his time in Carthage that Cato became resolute in the goal of destroying the city because he knew it was the greatest rival of the Roman Empire. Focusing the rest of his life on destroying Carthage, Cato is remembered today for ending every speech he made before the Roman Senate with, *"Carthago delenda est!"* ("Carthage must be destroyed!"). The Carthaginians wreaked havoc in the Mediterranean world and posed a constant threat to the expansion of *Pax Romana*, Roman peace. The Romans battled the Carthaginians in three massive wars called the Punic Wars, which eventually ended in the capture and total destruction of Carthage in The Third Punic War (149-146 B.C). The Romans were so determined to defeat Carthage that they made sure nothing was left alive by spreading salt over its ruins.

Cato's constant reminder of the threat from Carthage kept Rome focused on its ultimate purpose and led to Rome's greatest triumph—the destruction of the Carthaginians.

———◦◦◦———

Identifying the Purpose of Your Cold Call

Like Cato in the Punic Wars, sellers need to identify their ultimate objectives and stay focused on fulfilling those objectives. Before making cold calls, sellers need to ask themselves, "What is the purpose of my prospecting call? Is it to set up an appointment, or am I trying to discover whether or not there is a valid reason to set up an appointment in the first place?"

Good sellers will identify a purpose before making a cold call. For example, if you are a local life insurance agent and the sole purpose for cold calling is to set up face-to-face appointments, then the more cold calls the better. If someone is willing to meet with you eye-ball-to-eyeball, fantastic! On the other hand, if you are a *distance* seller located in San Francisco, California, selling software solutions across a northeastern territory that includes the states of Maine and Massachusetts, setting up face-to-face appointments without first qualifying prospects is sales suicide. Obviously, different prospecting objectives require different cold calling strategies; therefore, as the aim of each cold call varies, sellers must adapt their approaches accordingly. Cookie-cutter cold calling approaches simply won't cut it.

Two Types of Prospecting Calls

There are two types of prospecting calls:

1. Appointment-based calls
2. Qualification-based calls

I consulted with an executive who was setting up an internal call center, and when I asked him what kind of prospecting calls he was attempting to make, he gave me a blank stare. I then clarified my question, "Are you attempting to qualify accounts or set appointments?" While technically his answer of "both" was accurate, it failed to identify the purpose of the *initial* prospecting call. After a lengthy white board discussion, we determined that his objective was not to set appointments but to qualify accounts prior to passing them to his more senior salespeople. After a cold caller qualified a lead, a packet of information would be sent to the buyer, and the account data would be transferred to the appropriate salesperson. Later in the sales cycle, the sales representative would set an appointment for a capability demonstration, product presentation, or sales meeting.

Why is the distinction between appointment-based cold calls and qualification-based cold calls important to understand? Because, without first identifying the objective of your call, it isn't possible to create or utilize a consistent opening statement or cold call script. In addition, if you are a distance seller who uses "trains, planes, and automobiles" to travel through your territory, you will waste time and money attending appointments with prospects who are not qualified to purchase. The distinction is critical.

> **The Point?** Typically, the purpose of cold calling for local sales professionals is to set appointments. The opposite is normally true for distance sellers. The purpose of cold calling for distance sellers is to qualify accounts prior to appointments.

Appointment-based Cold Calls

If your cold call objective is to set an appointment, regardless of the qualifications of the account, then you are engaged in appointment-based cold calling. If a potential client agrees to meet with you face-to-face, at a specific time, you have succeeded. If, however, the potential client does not agree to meet with you face-to-face, at a specific time, you have not succeeded. Consequently, the success or failure of the call hinges strictly upon whether or not an appointment is set.

The appointment-based cold call is a simpler and faster sales call than a qualification-based cold call since appointment-based cold calls make no attempt to qualify the account over the phone. There are little-to-no qualifying questions asked, and once a potential client agrees to meet, the purpose of the call is completed. At that point, the seller says, "Thank you very much. I will see you on Tuesday at 9:00" and hangs up.

> **Note:** Keep in mind that appointment-based sellers eventually qualify prospects but not until the face-to-face meeting. The qualification process is *not* done on the phone. It's done at the appointment.

A sales training participant who sells high-end networking solutions once asked me, "Why on earth would a salesperson set up an appointment with an account that's not qualified?" While this may seem like an obvious question, in many cases cold calling is counter intuitive because it's really not as cut and dried as it first appears. For many sellers, it makes perfect sense to set up appointments with prospects who are not qualified prior to the appointment because the cost of the appointment is low, and the potential payoff is high. Sometimes qualifying an account face-to-face, versus on the phone, increases the probability of the sale.

A close friend of mine sells mortuary services that give his clients a complete plan for death. He sets up a financial plan to pay for the casket, the mortuary costs, the funeral expenses, the plot, and everything needed in case of a death in order to prevent people from passing on financial burdens to their families when they die. It's actually quite a responsible action for people to take. When my friend contacts people, his sole objective is to set up appointments. He does not bother attempting to qualify them prior to the presentation. Who could blame him? Can you imagine the questions he would need to ask in order to qualify an account prior to setting up an appointment? "Hi Ms. Jones, this is Bob from Fred's Mortuary. We were wondering if anyone in your family is preparing to die? (Response)... And is Mr. Jones going to die soon as well? (Response)... Good. Were you planning on selecting caskets together or separately? (Response). And how do you normally fund purchasing things like caskets and burial graves?"

There are some sellers who should not qualify accounts over the phone. For evident reasons, insurance agents, business consultants, and financial planners primarily engage in appointment-based cold calls.

> **Note:** A face-to-face sales meeting is the most effective way to make a sale, bar none. The best and most efficient way to set up a face-to-face sales meeting is through teleprospecting.

Qualification-based Cold Calling

Qualification-based cold calls have an entirely different objective than appointment-based cold calls. (The qualification process is discussed in detail in Chapter 10). The purpose of the qualification-based cold call is not to set up an appointment, but to qualify the prospect *prior to the appointment*. Because of the opportunity costs involved in distance selling, distance sellers cannot afford to run across a territory and speak with anyone and everyone willing to meet with them. Neglecting to qualify an account will waste the most precious and irreplaceable commodity known to man: time. Sellers must determine certain qualifications about buyers prior to setting appointments:

1. Ultimate Decision-maker(s) (UDM)
2. Available Funding
3. Appropriate Timeframe(s)
4. Matching Needs

One method of determining qualification after the initial opening statement is for the seller to focus on discovery-qualification questions to ensure matching needs between the product or service and the potential client. After the buyer explains a few account details, the seller asks qualifying questions such as:

- "Aside from yourself, who else will be involved in the decision making process?" (Ultimate Decision-makers).
- "How do you normally fund a project like this?" (Funding).
- "Mr. Prospect, assuming there's a good fit, what sort of timeframe would you be looking at to implement a project like this?" (Timeframe).

> **Note:** Qualification-based cold calls typically deal with high value, business-to-business products and services that are not purchased in a single sales call or meeting.

For many sales organizations, it makes sense to have full time cold callers "bird dog" qualified leads for sales representatives. Many sales organizations hire cold callers to qualify accounts prior to passing them on to more seasoned or experienced sales professionals. In this manner, more skilled sales personnel remain engaged in the latter, sometimes more difficult, stages of the sales cycle. Seasoned sales professionals posses skills and expertise associated with making difficult presentations or in-depth product demonstrations, so filling their pipelines for them with qualified leads through teleprospecting employees is most profitable.

The primary difference between appointment and qualification-based cold calling is this—appointment-based cold calls advance the buyer from the prospecting stage of the sales cycle to the investigation stage of the sales cycle in a face-to-face meeting *after the cold call* while qualification-based cold calls advance the buyer from the prospecting stage of the sales cycle to the investigation stage of the sales cycle *during the phone call.*

In Summary

The objective of the appointment-based cold call is to set up face-to-face meetings with potential clients at specific times; whereas, the objective of the qualification-based cold call is to qualify accounts prior to investing significant amounts of time, money, and effort. Sellers must be sure to identify the primary purpose of their prospecting efforts before making cold calls.

part two

II

OPENING THE CALL

CHAPTER 7

Opening the Prospecting Call

⸺➤●◄⸺

In 51 B.C., the king of Egypt, Ptolemy XII, died, leaving behind four potential heirs to the throne. By tradition, the eldest son, Ptolemy XIII, who was only 10 years old at the time, married his elder sister, Cleopatra, who was 18, and the two of them ruled Egypt as husband and wife. Since none of the Ptolemy heirs was satisfied with the situation, each vied for more power and a struggle emerged between Cleopatra and Ptolemy XIII as each tried to take command. In 48 B.C., Ptolemy XIII gained the support of the Egyptian government and forced Cleopatra to flee the country, leaving himself as sole ruler of Egypt. While in exile, Cleopatra schemed to restore Egypt to its glory days knowing that her brother was too weak to accomplish such a task.

Within months of Cleopatra's banishment, Roman dictator Julius Caesar, sensing the political vulnerability of Egypt, sought to make Egypt a Roman colony. News of Caesar's arrival in her country emboldened Cleopatra as she saw an opportunity to bypass the Egyptian bureaucracy and regain her lost power. Traveling hundreds of miles in disguise, and, as legend has it, reentering Egypt smuggled inside of a rolled up carpet, the young queen was gracefully revealed at Caesar's feet as the carpet was unfurled for the powerful dictator. Cleopatra immediately poured her feminine charm on Caesar, seducing him in order to support her cause.

Outraged that Cleopatra had outmaneuvered them, Ptolemy and his siblings summoned a great army and attacked Caesar in Alexandria. Although Caesar was caught off guard and narrowly escaped, he eventually repelled the attack. In the chaos of retreat, Ptolemy drowned while crossing the Nile.

Cleopatra married her 11 year-old brother, Ptolemy XIV, to reinforce her position as the uncontested queen of Egypt even though she was the lover of Caesar, to whom she bore a son named Caesarion. Mysteriously,

Ptolemy XIV died four years after his marriage to his older sister.

When Caesar died in 44 B.C., Cleopatra's power was once again vulnerable, and she knew that her only hope of survival was to maintain her alliance with Rome. Exercising the same charm and stratagem she used on Caesar, she seduced Roman general, Marc Antony. Antony fell deeply in love with Cleopatra (the couple had three children) and used his political and military power to protect her until 31 B.C. when he was defeated by the first emperor of Rome, Caesar Augustus.

A woman of great intelligence, Cleopatra ruled Egypt for almost twenty years, making the most of her physical charms to strengthen her control of Egypt. Her most significant political calculation, however, was bypassing the bureaucrats of the Egyptian government and going straight for the pinnacle of power to achieve her objectives. Rather than collaborating with the existing Egyptian government, she sought the support of the most powerful men in the world at the time: Julius Caesar and Marc Antony.

———⊰⊙⊱———

Choosing Your Point of Contact

Like Cleopatra's decision to bypass the Egyptian bureaucracy and instead immediately go for the apex of power, determining where to open a business-to-business sales call is not a trivial matter.

Questions about sales calls abound: where is the best place to open a sales call in a traditional business organization; are there rules about where to initially open a sales call? Are there dangers associated with initiating contact too low in a business hierarchy?

Choosing a point of contact needs to be a well thought-out decision. Beginning a call too low in a business hierarchy, for example, can waste time and link sellers to non-decision-makers. Beginning too high, on the other hand, can slam a sale shut if a seller is unprepared or speaks to an executive without a clear understanding of the company's needs and problems.

In complex, committee-based sales, sellers need to take the time to learn who the players are, what the prevailing view of the competition is, and how the proposed offering can solve specific customer problems.

I had a listener call my radio show, *The Business America Radio Show*, and state that while attempting to get his foot in the door of a major financial firm, he decided to go right for the jugular and call the president. To his surprise, when he phoned the company, the receptionist answered and immediately put him on the phone with the CEO. My listener gave his usual opening statement and made a few remarks, but it wasn't enough. The CEO showed no interest in his product and hung up. That caller is probably still kicking himself for wasting such a fantastic opportunity. Unfortunately, his mistakes are clear. Without sufficient preparation, he chose to initiate contact at the pinnacle of power without first establishing a strong foundation that demonstrated a clear need for his product. He couldn't be specific. He couldn't drop names and situations that would have piqued the interest of the CEO.

> **Note:** The general guideline is to start the initial sales call *high* on small, owner-run businesses and *low* on larger accounts that involve more than one decision maker.

When a good seller calls the CEO of a major corporation, he or she doesn't go in "half cocked." You need to be fully prepared and your target needs to be clear and specific because you will only get one chance. What the caller should have done was make a few lower level calls to talk to the people on the actual line of fire to identify their problems and uncover their dissatisfactions. Sellers should obtain the names of a few players and build internal champions to promote their product by conducting pre-call reconnaissance.

If this caller had done his homework prior to going straight for the CEO, he could have stated, "I spoke to Mary down in technical support, and she mentioned X problem. In fact, your I.T. director John Smith said he is experiencing the same problem." Questions about rudimentary business issues bore executives who view them as a waste of time, but when you catalogue exact names and specific problems, you gain their attention. More than likely, you will also be rewarded with an appointment with the right person.

When dealing with large, high-value accounts, I recommend *not* going straight to the zenith of power without adequate preparation. If you don't know the organization's pains and problems, the probability of making a compelling impact on an executive is unlikely.

> **Note:** Gaining immediate access to decision-makers is difficult, so don't waste the opportunity when you get it. Do your homework, and be prepared.

The Two-Step Approach

After experimenting with dozens of cold calling strategies, I have discovered numerous effective approaches to cold calling, but the two most effective cold calling methods that I use are the two and three step approaches.

In the two-step strategy, a seller uses pre-call correspondence to warm up buyers before making the actual cold call, building recognition and credibility prior to the call.

The first step of the two-step approach is to write a letter or send an email that briefly introduces the value of the offered product or service. Because of the prevalence of email Spam, I prefer sending both an email and formal letter. The initial letter provides buyers with convincing reasons to meet with the seller by outlining how the proposed product or service has benefited other clients as well as establishing the next point of contact by giving the buyer the exact follow-up date and time. (See a sample pre-call letter below).

Sample Pre-Call Letter

April 9, 2006

Mr. Brent Noorlander
Chief Executive Officer
SunQuest Technologies
1503 Jefferson Ave.
Seattle, Washington

Dear Mr. Noorlander,

Since implementing our advanced sales and negotiation trainings, both ABC Corporation and XYZ Company increased sales revenue over 15%.

Through our corporate sales training, we equipped their salespeople with the skills and strategies to make more sales, increase productivity, and most importantly, improve the bottom line.

We are confident that we will realize similar results for your organization.

I will follow up with you by telephone on Tuesday, April 15th at 9:00 A.M.

Sincerely,

Zac Fenton

Zac Fenton
Patrick Henry & Associates, Inc.
1 (877) 204-4341
zfenton@PatrickHenryInc.com

When you compose pre-call letters, send something creative and original that makes you stand out from your competitors. A training graduate related to me how using a creative two-step approach helps him set appointments. Prior to making cold calls, he mails introductory letters that contain a plastic zip lock bag with a crisp dollar bill in it. Referencing the dollar bill in his letter, he uses it as a way to introduce his method for saving the company money. His technique is so effective that when he follows up with a telephone call, his prospects know exactly who he is and mention the dollar bill to him. His creative pre-call approach gives him a much higher response percentage than his competitors who use traditional prospecting methods.

I know an extremely successful salesperson who uses a unique pre-call approach to sell radio advertisements. He produces radio ads for targeted clients and edits the ads to sound as if they are actually on the air. He burns the ads to individual CD's and mails them to targeted accounts. A few days later he follows up with a phone call and asks them how they like "their" radio advertisement. Since implementing this strategy his sales have increased exponentially.

You might send a potential buyer poker chips with the message, "Don't gamble on something as important as [accounting software]" or mail a tennis ball with a note that says, "Call me when your current supplier drops the ball"—anything that generates interest in a creative, professional way is a good idea.

When sharing some of these creative approaches, I have observed some trainees rolling their eyes as if to say, "Oh, puh-leeze." I've pointedly asked, "Is this too risky for you?" We must remember to test creative approaches by being as clever as Newton. Good sellers are always ready to embrace new truth even if it flies in the face of their pre-conceived notions. Remember, if it works, it may be repeatable, so put your emotion aside and test it.

Never lose sight of the fact that regardless of what method you choose to gain favorable attention, the goal is to set the all-important first interview.

> **Note:** Many salespeople find it useful to handwrite addresses on envelopes and use stamps instead of postage meters in order to personalize the look and feel of the letter and to improve the odds of the correspondence being read.

The Three-Step Cold Call Approach

My first sales job involved a mammoth amount of cold calling, and I quickly learned that the traditional method of cold calling our company recommended was ineffective. Instead of just dialing cold, I decided to fax prospects a short, personalized letter that introduced our company and product in addition to stating that I would be calling in a few days to follow up. In the letter I also included customer testimonials. (See Chapter 18 for more details about using client testimonials). I followed up the fax a day or two later by calling in the early morning or late evening when I was certain the prospect wouldn't be in, and leaving a voice message. My voice message stated that I wanted to confirm that they had received my faxed letter, briefly summarized the initial letter, and mentioned that I would be calling again; thus, this voice message placed my name in front of the prospect a second time before my actual call. The call didn't take place until step three, and I found that at that point, clients were reasonably comfortable with my call because I had already provided general introductory information.

In other cases, it makes sense to send more than one letter before making the follow-up call. For example, I know a salesperson who sends a series of notes and letters, containing testimonials from satisfied customers, over a two-week period to illustrate the benefits his product provides similar clients. In his final letter, he introduces himself and mentions a forthcoming follow-up call. In many cases buyers are so impressed with his correspondence that they actually call him before he calls them!

> **Note:** Remember that the primary goal of pre-call correspondence is to sell an interview with the prospect. It is not about selling the product or service itself.

Utilizing "Executive Assistants" to Set Appointments and Qualify Leads

When Julius Caesar invaded Britain in 55 B.C., his Roman soldiers encountered Celtic warriors skilled in chariot warfare who would attack their opponents by maneuvering their chariots close enough to their enemies to hurl javelins and shoot arrows. They would then leap from their chariots to fight hand to hand with broadsword, axe, and shield. When wearied from battle, the Celtic warrior would whistle to be picked up by his servant (called a charioteer) whose speed and skill in maneuvering the chariot was often the difference between life and death.

Whenever possible, sellers should use executive "charioteers" to make cold calls on their behalf. Using an executive assistant establishes power in the buyer-seller relationship, creates an image of success, and gives the impression that the salesperson is not desperate for business.[1] Instead, it communicates that the seller is a powerful executive who is in high demand.

Executive assistant calls are especially effective when used to make follow-up calls to direct mail letters. A sales assistant might follow up a

---

1. See Chapter 3 in *Sales-Side Negotiation* to learn more about the importance of building, maintaining, and exercising power in buyer-seller relationships.

letter by saying, "Hi Ms. Morgan, this is Mr. Hansen's executive assistant, Mary McKay. I'm calling to schedule an appointment between you and Mr. Hansen to discuss the topics addressed in the letter you recently received from us." This approach establishes a position of power and builds the image and reputation of the seller.

CHAPTER 8

Getting Past Gatekeepers

P.T. Barnum became America's premier showman in the nineteenth century. He started his career as an assistant to the owner of a traveling circus, Aaron Turner. On one of their tours, they stopped in Annapolis, Maryland, where Barnum decided to go for a walk in a new black suit that the circus owner purchased for him before one of his performances. As he strolled confidently through the city, a large crowd started following him, growing larger as he continued his walk. After turning a few corners and picking up his pace, Barnum grew nervous and turned and faced the crowd. A man suddenly shouted out, "It's the Reverend Ephraim K. Avery!" Reverend Avery had recently been acquitted on the charge of murder but the public still believed he was guilty. Barnum attempted to calm the crowd, not knowing who Reverend Avery was; however, the angry mob ripped Barnum's suit from his body and prepared to lynch him. Desperate to declare his innocence and his identity, Barnum convinced the crowd to follow him to the circus where he could verify his identity.

As the crowd approached the circus, Aaron Turner came out to meet them. He began laughing at the mob and confirmed that it was all a practical joke. Turner himself was responsible for buying the new suit and spreading the rumor that Barnum was the Reverend Avery. For good reason, Barnum was not amused by the joke, and after the crowd dispersed, he confronted his boss. After all, he had nearly been killed and had experienced the scare of his life. "My dear Mr. Barnum," replied Turner, "it was all for our good. Remember, all we need to ensure success is notoriety."

That night, the circus was packed with people as the entire town showed up anxious to see the people responsible for the joke. Barnum was amazed at the publicity the joke generated and learned a valuable lesson about the power of creative marketing. The showman never forgot this lesson, and throughout his career, he used clever marketing tactics and wholly unique publicity strategies to attract audiences. He went on to become one of the most renowned entertainers in United States history.

⟶⟫●⟪⟵

The Key to Getting Past Gatekeepers

I had a training graduate communicate an experience setting up an appointment with the CEO of a major account that illustrates the importance of using innovative selling methods. Unable to get past the gatekeeper, he decided to use a creative technique he had used in high school to get dates. He sent the gatekeeper a handwritten note sealed in a Ziploc bag frozen in the middle of an ice block. Because of the thickness of the ice, the message was opaque, but once the ice melted, the gatekeeper opened the Ziploc bag and read a message that said, "Now that we've broken the ice, any chance I can meet with you and Mr. Smith for lunch next Thursday?" He was awarded the appointment.

Because traditional methods for getting past gatekeepers don't work very often, sellers need to be creative and, like P.T. Barnum, sometimes do the *extra*ordinary to generate interest, get past gatekeepers and set appointments.

Gatekeeper Defined

I hear the word *gatekeeper* kicked around at every sales seminar I conduct or attend, but the term *gatekeeper* has a variety of definitions. For the sake of clarity and understanding, when I use the term gatekeeper, I am referring to *people who can say, "No"* by hanging up the phone or penciling you out of an appointment, *but they can't say, "Yes"* because they don't have power to authorize a sale. Not everyone in an organization can make a decision, but many individuals can pull the plug on your opportunity to sell.

> **Note:** It is a mistake to envision gatekeepers as strictly secretaries or receptionists (sometimes referred to as filters). A gatekeeper can be anyone who limits your ability to do business with ultimate decision makers.

Gatekeepers are usually pleasant and professional, and they can be instrumental to winning a sale because they have tremendous influence on the decision-making process by deciding who gets consideration. Without the assistance of a gatekeeper, you may not get the opportunity to sell because gatekeepers often control scheduling planners and appointment books.

Treat Gatekeepers with Respect

The first rule for getting past a gatekeeper is to treat him or her with respect. Good sellers recognize that many sales are lost when gatekeepers mention to a decision maker: "I didn't really like this guy. He was a first class jerk!" If you are rude or pompous to gatekeepers, they may say things about you to decision makers that will leave a negative impression of your character, your conduct, and even your product or service.

> **Caution!** Many sellers treat gatekeepers with disguised contempt—big mistake! Treat gatekeepers with dignity and respect rather than as roadblocks to be shoved out of the way.

Does this mean you should spend a great deal of time developing long-term relationships with gatekeepers? Probably not. In fact, in most cases getting too close to gatekeepers is a mistake, especially non-secretarial or non-administrative gatekeepers, because once engaged, you are typically "married" to them, which can severely limit your ability to navigate toward decision-drivers. If, however, you attempt to maneuver around the gatekeeper to access a decision-maker, you run the risk of alienating a convert. By jumping over the head of a gatekeeper, you can turn a potential ally into an enemy.

Qualify Your Point of Contact

During my rookie year in corporate sales, I worked on a major account in the most remote area I've ever visited—Bethel, Alaska. I arrived in Bethel on a one engine, "puddle jumper" airplane that seated six people. Unfortunately for the rest of the passengers, they didn't supply me with a convenient little vomit bag.

I was selling educational technology to a school district with a student population that was 90 percent Eskimo, many whose parents lived by subsistence hunting and fishing. Because of the high Native American population, the district received large amounts of federal funding for education, and every educational vendor knew it. It was a highly competitive sale. The district was composed of close to thirty schools, some located on islands with less than ten students who were taught in their native language until they were eight years old, at which time they were taught English. Amazingly, school supplies were airlifted in with district-owned one and two engine airplanes, so the district was highly interested in technology that could connect the various schools via a wide area network, allowing the schools to share information, communicate by email, and distribute electronic books and literature.

Initially, I worked almost exclusively with an I.T. coordinator to acquire technical and account information, and he supplied me with the data I needed to understand the account dynamics while also arranging dates and times for meetings and presentations. I worked closely with this gentleman and we developed an excellent relationship. The sale looked promising, but there was just one problem: this man had no decision-making authority. Just days before the presentation to the committee, he informed me that, although he was a commit-tee member, he had no voting privileges. I almost fell off of my chair. When I immediately began working directly with some of the people in the decision making body who were employed at the district level, I went over my initial contact's head, and he resented it.

Fortunately, I won the sale and learned an important lesson: good sellers qualify their point of contact. In business-to-business and committee-based sales, don't get married to specific account players simply because they are willing to spend time with you on the phone. Rather, carefully select, prior to your call whenever possible, where you are going to invest time and with whom. Choosing your point of entry and maneuvering yourself to decision drivers prior to having a non-decision maker put a ring on your finger will avoid your wasting time and effort as well as resentment when you go over the non-decision maker's head.

The general rule when opening a sales call is to contact the highest decision maker possible. Dealing with "C" level executives (CEO, CFO, CTO, COO, CIO, etc.) ensures that you interact with people who can put ink on paper, so find and interact with decision drivers, not gatekeepers.

> **The Point?** The best way to avoid alienating an influencer by going over his or her head is to initiate contact with the right person to begin with.

Remember that gatekeepers and other potential non-decision makers can be excellent sources of information *prior* to calling an executive. If a seller is unfamiliar with the needs or problems of a potential client, contacting a few people to gather information before talking to a decision maker can be extremely useful.

Getting Past the Gatekeeper

When you reach a gatekeeper instead of a decision maker, it is important to recognize what changed. What changed was the level of the sale. A sale must still be made, just to a different person. Sometimes you must first sell to the gatekeeper, which can take as little as sixty seconds, or it can take multiple calls. In many cases, sellers have to give a similar product or sales pitch to multiple people within an organization just to get to the right person. Don't let this discourage you. It is a normal part of selling in business-to-business sales where there are often multiple tiers in the selling process, even within a single account.

The Question-Question Strategy

One fairly effective technique for reducing the number of screening questions, and getting through to a decision maker, is the question-question strategy. When a gatekeeper asks screening questions, rather than offering traditional responses that all secretaries and administrative assistants are trained to recognize and block, answer the question with a question. For example:

Gatekeeper:	Good morning, ABC Widgets.
Seller:	Hi, may I speak with Ms. Jones please?
Gatekeeper:	May I tell her who is calling?
Seller:	Would you tell her you have Laura Olsen on hold please?
Gatekeeper:	Who are you with Ms. Olsen?
Seller:	Would you please tell her I am with *Patrick Henry & Associates*?
Gatekeeper:	What is this in reference to Ms. Olsen?
Seller:	Would you please tell her that I am calling with regard to sales training?

The question-question strategy is designed to prevent the gatekeeper from asking her next screening question and to keep her from saying "No" since it would be terribly awkward for the gatekeeper to say "No" to any of the recommended questions.

Of course, the question-question strategy will not eliminate all screening questions or work 100 percent of the time, but it will increase your chances of getting past gatekeepers.

Remember that in some cases, it is difficult to get past gatekeepers precisely because some gatekeepers, such as secretaries and administrative assistants, are professionally trained to screen calls, specifically solicitation calls. After you have banged your head a few times trying to get through, try something different or move on.

Seven Steps to Getting Past Gatekeepers

———⟫●⟨———

President John Quincy Adams, an enthusiastic swimmer, used to bathe naked in the Potomac River before starting the day's work. The newspaperwoman Anne Royall had been trying for weeks to get an interview with the President and had always been turned away. One morning she tracked him to the riverbank and after he was in the water stationed herself on his clothes. When Adams returned from his swim, he found a very determined lady awaiting him. She introduced herself and stated her errand. "Let me get out and dress" pleaded the President, "and I swear you shall have your interview." Anne Royall was adamant she wasn't moving until she had the President's comment on the questions she wished to put to him. If he attempted to get out, she would scream loud enough to reach the ears of some fishermen on the next bend. She got her interview while Adams remained decently submerged in the water.

———⟫●⟨———

As Anne Royall's example illustrates, dogged determination can be a salesperson's best ally. Her strategy of contacting President Adams on his morning swim is similar to recommendation number five for getting past gatekeepers: contact decision makers at off-peak hours.

The following behaviors will increase your likelihood for success, regardless of how difficult it may be to get past some gatekeepers:

1. *Sell the gatekeeper.* On major accounts, send a personalized letter, note, or email directly to the gatekeeper. Sell the gatekeeper and you

won't have a problem gaining access to the primary decision maker. You might say to the gatekeeper, "Tammy, I'd like to make a deal with you. I would like to review our product with you. If what I present to you is not acceptable and you know it won't fly, just tell me so and I'll be on my way. If you like what I present and feel it will benefit your company, all I ask is that you allow me to represent myself to the president. Is that fair?"

Never forget the power of creativity. During our trainings, I encourage salespeople to relate stories about experiences they have had getting past gatekeepers. I have had training participants do something as simple as sending a gatekeeper a pack of pencils with his or her name imprinted on it to something as extravagant as sending a basket of European cheese and a bottle of wine including a note that reads, "I hope this isn't 'cheesy' or sound like I am 'whining,' but I would love to talk to you and Mr. Smith about X." Some sellers find that sending gatekeepers items like gift certificates to local restaurants, movie passes, concert tickets, gift baskets, or other inexpensive items is extremely effective. I read of a salesperson who sent a gatekeeper a box of Minute Rice with a handwritten note that said, "I would like to meet with Mr. Jones when he can find a minute."

Simply put, if you are serious about getting past a gatekeeper, you must first sell the gatekeeper.

2. Ask for help. Solicit the assistance of the gatekeeper with "help" questions such as, "I was wondering if you could help me please?" "Perhaps you can help me?" or "I need your help." My personal favorite is "What would you do if you were me to get an appointment with Ms. So-and-so?" You might say to the gatekeeper, "Sandra, my name is Eric Mostetler and I need your help. What are the criteria I must meet to have an audience with the CEO?" These questions are powerful tools to generating assistance rather than resistance from gatekeepers.

3. Be polite. Rudeness will get you nowhere. Keep in mind that many sales are slammed shut by disrespectful, "off the cuff" remarks intended to put gatekeepers "in their place."

4. Be honest. Nobody likes being manipulated, so don't try to manipulate the gatekeeper. By telling gatekeepers your objective, you make them part of your team, so tell them the truth and ask them how you can get an appointment.

5. Call at off-peak hours or on Saturdays. Because decision makers often work when gatekeepers don't, you should call at a time when the prospect is likely to be in, but the gatekeeper isn't. The best times are early morning—7:00 A.M.; Lunchtime—noon to 1:00 P.M.; or early evening—5:00 P.M. to 7:00 P.M. I know a company that sets aside early morning hours for cold calling specifically to bypass receptionists while other sellers strategically call after 5:00 P.M., knowing that potential gatekeepers typically go home at a scheduled time, but executives and managers often work late. In many industries, Saturday happens to be a pretty good day to reach heads of companies.

6. Be funny. Humor is still one of the greatest sales tools that exist. Being jovial and friendly makes people want to help you. You might start off by saying, "Ms. Jones, I know you actually run [business name], but could you put me through to the person who thinks they do?" Be creative, and use humor.

7. Ask for sales or marketing. If you are having a hard time getting past a gatekeeper, call and ask for the sales or marketing department because in many firms, receptionists are told not to give out any names except sales and marketing names. When you get through to the sales or marketing person, tell him or her who you are, what you do, what you are trying to accomplish, and who they recommend that you contact. If that doesn't work, ask for accounts receivable because no business turns down calls to accounts receivable. Once you get through, ask to be transferred to the person you are attempting to contact.

CHAPTER 9

Establishing a Powerful Telepresence

———⊰●⊱———

Johann Sebastian Bach, Wolfgang Amadeus Mozart, and Ludwig van Beethoven are three of the most accomplished composers in history. Each man made an indelible mark on classical music. They were German and lived in roughly the same era, but each of them orchestrated sounds and harmonies that were completely distinct and unique to his own personality. Bach, for example, was only five feet tall. Nevertheless, he had a giant intellect, passionate personality (he had twenty children), and an overpowering presence that was reflected in his music. A devoted Lutheran, he integrated his deep religious convictions into his melodies. He is perhaps best known for his composition, *Toccata and Fugue in D Minor for Organ.*

Mozart, unlike Bach, was foul-mouthed and socially distasteful. He had an odd fondness for shocking people with his love of swearing and uncouth behavior. He was, by traditional standards, unconventional, brilliant, and eccentric, as was his music. He created a distinct sound known for its mastery of form and richness of harmony. He composed symphonies, operas, concertos, sonatas, and choral and chamber pieces, and is credited with over six hundred works in his brief life (he died at the age of thirty-five). Mozart's most famous works include his *Serenade in G Major, Symphony No. 40 in G Minor, and Concerto No. 21 in C Major for Piano and Orchestra.*

Although Bach and Mozart created profound musical masterpieces, none can compare to Beethoven's *Symphony No. 5 in C Minor.* The combination of power and gentleness in the first movement of *Symphony No. 5* represents the most famous four notes in all of classical music—dot, dot, dot, dash. (Coincidentally, the rhythm of these four notes spells out V in Morse code and came to symbolize Victory during World War II). Beethoven's opening rhythm in *Symphony No. 5* is the most recognized classical phrase ever created.

Its distinct harmony and unique   is both captivating and engaging.
sound establishes a presence that

———⟫●⟪———

Making a Favorable Impression

Like the great composers of the past, modern sales professionals need
to establish a powerful presence and make a favorable impression early
in the buyer-seller relationship. For this reason, successful cold calls
must start with an effective opening statement that creates an immediate telepresence, the verbal and mental image evoked in the mind of a
buyer over the phone.

Think of the last cold call you received. What questions did you
ask yourself about the caller? What judgments did you make? Almost
like a gag reflex, the second we hear a seller on the phone we start forming opinions and asking ourselves questions such as:

Does this person sound friendly or pushy?

Does she sound natural or phony?

Is he reading from a script?

Does this person speak English?

Does she sound knowledgeable or like a minimum wage
telemarketer?

I received a call from a company trying to get me to subscribe to a
particular trade magazine. The caller was absolutely flawless. I listened
to her initial "pitch" and actually smiled as I listened to her tone and
formed a mental image of her sitting in her cubicle making calls. The
first point that struck me was her attitude, which was upbeat and optimistic. She could have been cold calling on behalf of Disneyland for
all I could tell. She was professional. Her language was appropriate and
intelligent. At the conclusion of her opening statement, I said to her,
"Young lady, you're good!" She laughed and then got right down to
business about the magazine subscription.

I had never seen or spoken to this person before. Still, I formed a mental image of her based on her voice, tone, and language and developed an impression of her personality in less than a minute. I even formed an image of what I thought she might look like. Admit it, we all do it.

I recently had a guest on my radio show walk into the studio and blurt out, "You look exactly as I imagined!" My voice, my tone, my language, and my personality created an image in the mind of my guest.

The same thing happens when we cold call. The young lady who sold me the magazine subscription created a telepresence that was mentally palpable. Her opening statement and attitude communicated that I could talk to her without getting pushed over a sales cliff or cajoled into a purchase. I was able to make this assessment in less than thirty seconds.

After subscribing to the magazine she was selling, I evaluated her call and jotted down a few notes. What was it about her call that made it so effective? Her success boiled down to two things:

1. The appeal of her opening statement
2. The favorable impression she created

In order to make a positive first impression, a favorable telepresence must be established. In other words, you need to sound attractive. You need to project an image and attitude that is positive and encouraging. Your tone and language should reflect optimism and confidence. For this reason, I recommend making business-to-business cold calls first thing in the morning before getting bogged down or tired by the trials of the day.

> **Note:** Being upbeat and cheerful is an important part of cold calling. People can sense the mood of a salesperson by the tone of his or her voice.

I managed a gentleman named David who was the most positive salesperson I've ever worked with. Always smiling and upbeat, this guy was constantly happy. I would walk by him in the hallway and ask, "How's it going?" He always responded with such statements as, "If I were any better, I wouldn't know what to do with myself!" I noticed that everyone, including me, would smile when he came down the hall. He projected genuine optimism, and his positive attitude affected everyone else's attitude, including buyers. He created a presence that was, to put it lightly, favorable. It wasn't a coincidence he was one of our top sellers.

Let me give you a personal example of how dangerous a bad attitude can be when cold calling. When I first started my sales consultation business, I spent each morning cold calling and setting up appointments to sell corporate sales training. On one particular morning I'd been at it for close to an hour with terrible results. It seemed like everyone I spoke to was rude, cold, or indifferent. Their negative attitudes started to wear on me, and led to a huge mistake. I called a lead that I had left two messages for in previous weeks. Because of information I had from a mutual associate, I knew that company needed what I offered but, as fate would have it, the receptionist put me into the decision makers' voice mail. I knew the decision maker was avoiding me. I then made a terrible mistake and left the worst voice message possible. I said, "Hi, this is Patrick Hansen again. I've already left you multiple voice messages. I think it's unprofessional of you not to return my calls. I will not be calling you again. If you would like to increase your sales, you need to call me."

I hung up the phone and sat there in stunned silence, reflecting upon what I had just done. I'll venture to say that decision maker didn't create a favorable mental or emotional image of me after listening to my voice mail. I could not believe that Mr. Cerebral Salesman himself had just done something so stupid. Needless to say, I never received a call back, and in fact, months later I ran into the associate who gave me his name in the first place. I wanted to crawl in a sewer hole when he informed me that he had heard what I had done. I assume that I will never get another referral from that man again and who could blame him? I let my bad mood dictate my behavior.

| Caution! Bad moods kill good cold calls. |

Projecting an optimistic telepresence is critical to the success of the initial sales call, so if you are feeling angry, frustrated, or upset, stand up and take a short break. You might go for a quick, brisk walk or splash some cold water on your face. You must do something to eliminate your bad mood.

Phone Etiquette, Verbal Skills, and Appropriate Language

Before I jump into the pulp of a good cold call, let me review the importance of using appropriate phone etiquette, pronunciation, and verbal skills.

Appropriate phone etiquette is a mandatory element of successful prospecting and starts with the appropriate use of language and correct pronunciation of words. Using clear language and correct diction is not optional when cold calling. You may get by with poor verbal skills when getting directions on the streets of a downtown city, but it won't help you become a better, more productive cold caller in the business world.

The fastest way to frustrate a potential buyer is to speak in a way that is confusing, or unclear, or by using language a prospect can't understand. If you don't use appropriate, understandable language, you won't make a favorable impression with buyers.

You should avoid a number of annoying speech habits when cold calling:

- Sounding nasal
- Heavy breathing
- Mumbling
- Sounding monotone
- Using slang
- Excessive stuttering
- Long pauses

Your voice needs to be warm, friendly, and properly pitched. Avoid speaking too loudly, too softly, too quickly, or too slowly. Make sure that your words are not garbled or slurred. A great cold call script can be sabotaged with poor voice control, incorrect diction, or both.

When I discuss verbal skills and appropriate language, I am not referring to foreign or regional accents. As long as people can understand you, accents are positive. People love to hear accents, and they sometimes lead to personal discussions about geographic locations (such as north or south), nationality, or national origin. All of us have had people with accents call us. Most of the time we inquisitively ask, "So where are you from?"

> **The Point?** Opening statements either open doors or slam them shut. The telepresence you establish and the mental image you create in the first sixty seconds of a cold call can make or break the remainder of a sales conversation.

Prospecting Scripts

Effective opening statements don't happen by accident. They are thought out, rehearsed and practiced. Because effective opening statements don't just happen, it's important to create a prospecting script prior to cold calling.

Elite sellers use scripts when they prospect. Some read the script, in a conversational tone, of course, while others only reference the script. Some sellers simply have the script lying on their desk as a handy backup in case they get stuck. My point is that they don't rely on chance or luck to make a powerful opening statement. They don't count on their ability to come up with effective verbiage off the top of their heads. As every seasoned seller will tell you, it's impossible to be on your mental "A" game on every call.

> **Note:** Power prospectors understand that there are no second chances when it comes to cold calling. You get one shot to advance the sale. Scripts ensure that you make the most of the opportunity.

One of the advantages of selling over the phone is that you can use a script. I taught this principle to a sales team for a technology company where I was tasked with establishing a call center to generate qualified leads to pass to senior sales personnel. I spent a full day training and role-playing. In the group was a young college student whose confidence exceeded his intellect. After the training, he confided to me that although the other cold callers might need a script, he wouldn't (wink, wink). I didn't want to bruise his ego or crush his enthusiasm, so I said nothing. A few hundred calls later, he was using a script. After being drilled by astute buyers, getting flustered, verbally lost, and mentally shot down a few times, he didn't think using a cold call script was bad after all.

Many sellers are reluctant to use scripts for fear of sounding "canned." That's understandable. No one wants to sound like he or she is reading from a piece of paper. This is why it is important to memorize and mentally internalize cold call scripts. By mastering your script, you will develop the ability to speak in a natural, comfortable way. One technique to conversationalize a cold call script is to practice it into a tape recorder or voice mail until it comes across as natural and unrehearsed.

> **Note:** There is an enormous difference between "canned" and "planned" prospecting scripts. Scripts that are memorized, referenced, and verbally rehearsed are planned. Scripts that are obviously read are canned.

Preparing a Prospecting Script

Developing an effective prospecting script takes preparation. It's like an Olympic athlete. Olympic sprinters and swimmers win gold medals in races that are won in seconds, not hours. Think of how much time it takes to prepare to run a 100-meter dash. The race is won in less than 10 seconds. How much preparation goes into winning the race? How many hours do athletes spend weight lifting, practicing, stretching, and running?

Karl Malone, the former All Star power forward for the Utah Jazz, publicly criticized his teammates for showing up to summer camp out of shape because he knows that what takes place in the off-season determines what takes place in the regular season. Selling is much the same. You need to prepare to be successful.

Scripts ensure that consistent cold call strategies are implemented. By going through the mental process of creating, editing, and rehearsing cold call scripts, sellers fine tune their messages. They develop key words and phrases and position key sentences for strategic moments in the phone call. (See Chapter 9 for a step-by-step example of creating a cold call script).

Furthermore, scripts give sellers confidence and provide a backup system should they become flustered. They can also be used to write down product notes, questions to ask, and/or responses to potential objections. (See Chapter 16 for effective rejoinders to common cold call responses).

Don't Prospect Without a Script

I refer to non-scripted prospecting as, "Mumbling, Stumbling, and Fumbling." Sellers who neglect to use a script end up not only rambling, but also using words and phrases that detract from the impact of the call because they inadvertently inject what are called "weasel words." Theodore Roosevelt coined this term to describe, "Words that destroy the force of a statement by equivocal qualification as a weasel ruins an egg by sucking out its content while leaving it superficially intact." Words such as "uh," "ah," "um," and "you know" are considered weasel words since they have no purpose and add no meaning to a conversation.

The Point? Don't prospect without a script. Scripts make cold calls more effective, persuasive, and successful. Unscripted cold calls are longer, wordier, less effective, and tend to stray from the point of the call.

CHAPTER 10

Creating a Power Benefit Statement

In the early stages of *World War II*, the Germans invaded Denmark and attempted to convert the Danish monarchy into a puppet government on behalf of the Third Reich. But one bold man stood in their way: the leader of Denmark, King Christian X. Although powerless to militarily defeat the German war machine, he did, nevertheless, attempt to thwart German efforts to recruit Danish men into the German army.

On the morning after German occupation, King Christian spotted a Nazi flag flying over a public building. Furious at the arrogance of the Nazis, King Christian summoned a German commander and ordered the removal of the flag. When the German commander refused, the king informed the German commander that if he did not remove the flag, he would order a Danish soldier to do so. The German commander made it clear that he would shoot any soldier who attempted to remove the flag. "I think not," said the seventy-three year old king, "because I will be the soldier." King Christian removed the flag.

Weeks later, the Germans ordered all Jews living in Denmark to wear a yellow armband so that they could be identified and searched by Nazi troops. The day after the order, King Christian emerged from his royal palace wearing a yellow armband. In open defiance of the Nazi order, King Christian went for his daily horseback ride wearing the yellow armband in public. Within days, the yellow armband was seen everywhere, becoming the most popular item sold in Denmark.

Tired of the king's defiance, Hitler ordered his arrest, and King Christian was forthwith removed from the palace and imprisoned. Seeing their king imprisoned was the last straw for the Danish populace. In the dark hours of the morning following King Christian's arrest, thousands of Danish men slipped out of their homes and cottages, made their way to the coasts of Denmark, and launched hundreds of fishing boats toward England to join the Allied forces.

⸺᚛●᚜⸺

The Power of Boldness

Everyone admires the bold; no one honors the timid.

—Robert Green

King Christian's courageous defiance of Nazi occupation is a great example of the power of boldness. King Christian did not deliver a stirring speech or print anti-Nazi flyers or pamphlets. He simply set an example by resisting the Nazis himself. He was bold, but he was gracefully bold. He chose not to be obnoxious or overbearing, just resolute and persistent in his brave but calm acts of defiance.

Obviously, being bold can be difficult, but it can also be rewarding—especially in sales. This is why one step of *The Power Benefit Statement* is to make a bold value statement. The bold value statement is not an obnoxious brag statement. It is an assertive declaration of achievement, and is, I believe, the most important step in *The Power Benefit Statement*. (See *Figure 9.2*).

The Power Prospecting Model

In order to fully exploit the prospecting stage of the sales cycle, it is important to use a clear and usable prospecting model. *The Power Prospecting Model* outlines the strategic steps of a cold call. It provides sellers with a clear methodology to make effective prospecting calls and consists of a unique selling proposition (see chapter 5), power benefit statement, *The DNASelling Method* (see chapter 11), and a commitment-based conclusion.

The Power Prospecting Model maps the cold calling process and ensures that sellers do not miss vital steps in the prospecting stage of the sales cycle. By utilizing *The Power Prospecting Model*, sellers enhance the quality of their cold calls and increase their call-to-close ratios.

The Power Prospecting Model

Unique Selling Proposition	A message based on the most unique product feature, service offering, or benefit capability.
↓	
Power Benefit Statement	The opening statement of a teleprospecting call that gains attention, generates interest, and advances the sale.
↓	
The DNASelling Method	A questioning methodology that follows a rational probing sequence for qualification-based cold calls.
↓	
Committment-Based Close	A closing strategy that gains mutual agreement to specific action and establishes the next step of the sales process.

Figure 10.1

Note: Developing a Unique Selling Proposition is addressed in Chapter 5.

The Power Benefit Statement

The second step of *The Power Prospecting Model* is the power benefit statement. The objective of the power benefit statement is to obtain the customers' consent to advance the call to the investigation stage of the sales cycle. In fact, the objective of every step of the sales process is to advance to the next step of the sales cycle. You want buyers to agree that it's legitimate for you to ask them questions or meet with them personally.

Since the early 1970's, opening cold call statements have been popular in the selling industry. To varying degrees, they have been effective. Salespeople have been trained to provide *Initial Benefit Statements, Implied Benefit Statements, Opening Benefit Statements, Direct Benefit Statements,* etc. These sales openers are often referenced by their acronyms IBS, OBS, and DBS. Unfortunately, some of them are just plain BS. Many opening sales statements are too long, too wordy, and too difficult to execute.

> **Note:** Effective opening cold call statements are tactical and concise. They are strategic, intelligent statements designed to generate interest, qualify leads, and set appointments in an interesting, brief, and powerful manner.

Effective opening cold call statements imply value, an implied *benefit* to the buyer for staying on the phone and engaging in a sales conversation. Thus, we refer to the opening cold call statement as a *Power Benefit Statement.* Using the Unique Selling Proposition that we addressed in Chapter 5, sellers are prepared to develop an opening statement that implies value to the buyer.

Your Thirty Second Commercial

Brevity is the soul of wit.

—William Shakespeare

A power benefit statement should be thirty seconds—never longer than forty-five seconds. Anything longer makes potential buyers antsy and frustrated. Longwinded cold calls force buyers to interrupt sellers just to get a word in. We've all experienced long-winded sales calls in which you literally wait for the seller to take a breath and then jump in and say, "Sorry, I'm not interested." We cut cold callers off because they talk too much and take too much time to get to the point.

I received a cold call from a real estate agent whose brevity was brilliant. He called and said,

> *"Hi Mr. Hansen, I'm John with ABC real estate. I sold your neighbor's home at 888 Willow Street. Are you or anyone you know looking to sell a home?"*

Granted, some cold calls are impossible to make this brief, especially business-to-business cold calls, but the point is to keep cold calls as concise as possible without compromising critical information.

Elongated, wordy messages are boring and ineffective. Make sure you can get through the opening statement at a reasonable pace in approximately thirty seconds. With a concise, power opening statement, you pique the interest of buyers without boring them.

Creating a Power Benefit Statement

There are five steps to the power benefit statement:

1. Introduce and identify yourself, your company, and (optional) your location
2. State a common reference
3. Make a bold value statement
4. State the purpose of your call
5. Listen

Many training participants have asked, "Do I really need all this to make a good cold call?" My answer is always a firm "Yes" because if you leave out or try to defer any of the recommended steps, you will not be as successful. It's really that simple. People want to know to whom they are talking, what the purpose of the call is, and why they should listen.

It is not a coincidence that the strategic benefit statement parallels the questions receptionists and secretaries ask when they receive unsolicited calls. "May I have your name please?" "Who are you with?" "What is this in reference to?"

> **Note:** Steps two, three, and four of the power benefit statement can be reversed, combined, or remain in that order. The primary concern is not that you use them in precise order but that you use them.

Step 1: Introduce and Identify Yourself, Your Company, and (optional) Your Location

The purpose of the first step of the cold call is to gain the buyer's attention and to preemptively answer questions about who you are, who you represent, and from where you are calling. You don't want these questions to linger in the back of the buyer's mind while engaged in conversation. Even though this sounds fundamental, I mention it for one reason—most cold callers do a poor job of early identification.

How many times have you had to ask a first time caller, "What is your name?" "Who are you with?" "Where are you calling from?" These are questions buyers should not have to ask after the first sentence of the opening statement.

Using the buyer's name to open the call is the most important, surest, and easiest way to gain the attention of a buyer. Names have power.

I learned the power of using a person's name in high school. My junior year I had a history teacher who perturbed me immensely (probably not nearly as much as I perturbed him). I did anything and everything I could to torment him. For instance, in the middle of his lectures I would raise my hand and ask him if he knew what Mr. Rogers' opinion was on the matter, or I would rearrange all of the desks before class (all facing the opposite direction of the chalk board of course). Placing his chair directly against his desk and gluing it to the floor didn't turn out to be a big plus for my GPA. You get the idea.

This particular history teacher was once walking down a very crowded hall in which students were everywhere scrambling to get to class. When this teacher approached, I stood up on my heels and yelled at the top of my lungs "Mr. SMITH!" Nobody in the hallway even noticed except him, and he turned his head in both directions, wondering who on Earth was calling his name. As soon as he would put his head down and start walking again, I would yell, "Mr. SMIIIITH!" He would stop and frantically, nervously look around. I repeated this process at least four or five times, and was amazed that he kept falling for it over and over. At the time, I surmised that his name was a magnet too powerful to ignore, even after he realized it was being called out for no purpose. Each time, it got his attention even when he realized it shouldn't have. My point is that using a person's name has a way of gaining a person's attention. As legendary author Dale Carnegie stated, "A man's name is to him the sweetest and most important sound in any language."

If you are calling from an information list that does not list the first or last name of the contact person, you have three options:

1. Say, "Hi this is (your name)" and skip mentioning his or her name.
2. Say, "Hi this is (your name), with whom am I speaking?"
3. Call ahead of time and ask for the name of the person with the title to whom you wish to speak.

A frequently asked question by training participants is, "Should I use a prospect's first or last name when I cold call?" "Should I say, 'Hi Bob' or 'Hi Mr. Jones?'" I typically respond to this question with a question. "Does it really make that much of a difference?" "Is a prospect not going to buy because someone called him Bob instead of Mr. Jones?" Our research indicates it's a moot issue; however, when in doubt, use Mr. or Ms.

After stating the contact's name, state your name and tell him or her who you are. If you don't feel comfortable giving your last name, then don't, but make sure you give them some point of reference and identification.

After stating your name, identify the name of your company and tell them who you represent. When sellers don't identify who they represent, suspicions are sometimes unnecessarily aroused, and prospects wonder why the caller doesn't just come out and state who they represent.

Just prior to the 2002 Winter Olympics in Salt Lake City, I received a cold call from the Salt Lake City Chamber of Commerce asking me if I wanted to place an ad in their Olympic directory. The caller had a fairly decent opening statement. He stated, "Hi Mr. Hansen. This is Scott from The Salt Lake Area Chamber of Commerce." It was nice and clean, and I knew exactly to whom I was speaking and what organization he represented.

Identifying your location is a little less cut and dried. Some sellers swear by it, but other sellers swear against it. I recommend the following rule when mentioning locations: *Only mention your location if it will pique the interest of the buyer and build credibility.* For example, mentioning that you are calling from Billings, Montana, probably isn't going to impress an executive in New York City. However, if you are selling western antiques to country stores, mentioning you are from Billings, Montana, might spark an interesting conversation.

I consulted with a software company that sells technical solutions to manufacturing facilities primarily in large, industrial cities. The location of the software company was nowhere near a major industrial city. When we started the cold calling process, we initially included the corporate location in the script. It was not a wise choice because many of the buyers would say things that insinuated that we couldn't possibly know what they needed if we weren't local or from a similar industrial city or state. Although the insinuations were false, it was like fighting the tide, so we took the location reference out of the script.

Caution! If used mindlessly or just out of habit, mentioning your location may actually hurt your sales call.

Sample Introductions

"Hi Mr. Prospect, this is Zac Fenton with Patrick Henry & Associates."

"Good afternoon Sharon, my name is Susan Graham. I'm with ABC Company here in Chicago. We also have offices in New York and Los Angeles."

"Hi Ms. Jones, my name is David Weaver. I'm a sales consultant with XYZ Company."

"Good morning Mr. Finnegan, this is Rachel with American Widgets calling from Cupertino, California."

Many sellers like to inject a greeting after introducing themselves. For example, "Hi Mr. Prospect, this is Tyler Hansen with *Patrick Henry & Associates. How are you today?"* Or, *"How is it going?"* I personally don't like to inject greetings. I believe that they come across as artificial and interrupt the flow of the opening benefit statement. However, many successful cold callers use greetings, so my recommendation is to do what feels the most comfortable and natural. However, in a purely professional sense, I would advise against it.

Step 2: State a Common Reference

Stating a common reference piques the interest of buyers. We are all interested in things, people, and organizations with whom we are familiar. For example, if you are the president of a bank and I mention the names of other banks I'm working with, you will more than likely be interested in what I have to say. If I am a life insurance agent and mention your neighbor across the street or a person you go to church with, you will more than likely perk up and listen. If you are a software distributor and I drop the names of major software companies I'm working with, you will take notice.

> **Note:** Using a common reference increases the curiosity and interest of the buyer.

Stating a common reference also establishes credibility early in the sales call. In every major industry, city, and market there are individuals and organizations that are recognized as industry or market leaders. If you work with recognized individuals or businesses, use them as common references.

Years ago, I consulted with a company working on a major sale. In fact, it was by far the largest sale they had ever tackled. We hammered on this sale every day for months using late night telephone strategy sessions, unexpected last minute flights, product adjustments, last minute RFP (request for proposal) changes, etc. We won the sale.

The organization that purchased the product was an industry-known name from a major city, so I advised the company with whom I was consulting to immediately insert the "win" into their prospecting scripts. We trained a team of full time cold callers to use the name of this particular buyer with every cold call. In other words, we injected a common reference.

Every person we contacted heard about this sale—every voice mail, every message. The cold callers would state that "ABC Corporation" recently purchased "X product." By using the name of this purchaser, we established instant credibility in the minds of buyers, and within six months, news of this particular sale swept the entire industry. We went a step further and announced the sale on the corporate web site, in magazine advertisements and literature, posting product testimonials and favorable quotes from the sale on industry "listservs." We made certain this sale was mentioned in every sales presentation by creating a PowerPoint presentation with quotes, testimonials, decision criteria, and competitive comparisons.

It worked fabulously. We utilized this sale to put a small to mid-sized company on the map. Within twelve months of the sale, this company grew into a dominant player that was literally feared by its competitors. None of this would have occurred had we not strategically exploited this major sale as a common reference in their prospecting and marketing efforts.Using a common reference has the dual effect of increasing interest and utilizing "herd theory." The fact that everyone else is moving in a certain direction implies that something about your offering is of value. People sometimes consider purchasing products and services based strictly on the fact that other reputable companies have already bought the products or services under consideration.

Another way to use a common reference is to use the name of a prospect's competitor. Every business knows their competition, so why not use a prospect's competitor as a common reference? Dropping the names of competitors can be remarkably effective in gaining the attention of buyers.

The more precise the common reference, the better. Avoid using vague references, and instead, use exact names. Names with an established presence or favorable reputation are powerful common references.

> **The Point?** Don't be afraid to exploit your successes. Use a recent win or recognizable client as a common reference. Broadcast your successes with current accounts that have name or brand recognition.

Sample Common References

"Hi Ms. Jones, this is Karl Tobler. I am a consultant with *Patrick Henry & Associates.*"

> *We've recently done a lot of work with software companies in the areas of cold calling and prospect management, most recently at ABC Company...*

> *We just completed working with XYZ Corporation in your area...*

> *The reason I'm calling today is because I just completed a very successful sales training with ABC Company here in Boston...*

We recently had XYZ Company out of Dallas, Texas purchase X product...

Some of our clients include ABC Corporation and XYZ Company...

Whenever I teach this principle, I inevitably have a "stump the chump" participant raise his hand and ask, "That's all good and dandy, Mr. Cerebral Salesman, but what if you are just starting a business or haven't yet landed any major accounts to use as a common reference?"

When in doubt, or if you don't have an existing clientele to use as a reputable common reference, use the following format to create an effective reference statement:

"Good afternoon Mr. Smith. My name is Mitch Nelson. I'm the director of marketing at *Patrick Henry & Associates.*"

> *We've recently been working with (market or industry). One of the primary concerns we hear from other (title) is their frustration with (problem) .*

For example:

> *"Good afternoon Mr. Smith. My name is Mitch Nelson. I'm the director of marketing at Patrick Henry & Associates. We've recently been working with (the banking industry). One of the primary concerns we hear from other (vice presidents) is their frustration with (the difficulty their loan officers have in closing qualified accounts)."*

To identify a common market problem to use as a common reference, make a list of the top five problems your product or service resolves. Determine which of the five is the most commonly experienced problem and use it. If buyers say, "I don't have that problem" you can use the remaining problems as a backup. For example, you might say, "Other problems we've helped our clients resolve are _____." The key is to focus the buyer's attention on critical issues and pressing problems that he or she may be experiencing.

Using a prospect's industry as a common reference builds interest, and mentioning similar or exact job titles piques attention. Additionally, stating industry-wide problems faced by other companies induces curiosity.

Step 3: Make a Bold Value Statement

Making a bold value statement projects confidence and is the greatest indicator of a seller's success. People who exude confidence instill confidence in others. When you show confidence in your company, product or service, it's noticeable. People recognize it and sense it. They feel by your words that you really believe in your company, good, or service. By making a bold value statement, you project certainty and eliminate doubt.

Bold value statements establish that you have a legitimate reason to talk to the buyer. You are calling because you have been able to help other clients, and you believe that your goods or services will be of the same help for them.

The primary purpose of the bold value statement is to imply value, and the best and quickest way to establish value is to reference the value you have provided other clients. By referencing a success story or making a bold statement of achievement, you give buyers a snapshot of the value you have offered other companies.

Implying value does not mean opening your call with a laundry list of capabilities, and I am not suggesting that you use the power benefit statement to verbally list every feature, capability, or benefit you offer. That would be an opening brag statement, not a power benefit statement.

> **The Point?** Associating a bold value statement with a common reference adds sting to the cold call. By making a bold statement of achievement, sellers project confidence and give buyers a compelling reason to listen.

Sample Bold Value Statements

"Good afternoon Mr. Smith. My name is Patrick Hansen. I'm the president of *Patrick Henry & Associates*. We do sales training for real estate companies. Some of our clients include ABC Corporation and XYZ Company. One of the primary concerns I'm hearing from other executives is their disappointment with real estate agents who struggle setting sales appointments."

> *The reason I am calling is because we just completed a very successful sales training with 123 Corporation. In fact, we helped increase their sales appointments by 25%...*
>
> *The purpose of my call is simply to set up a meeting to discuss ways in which we've been successful with other companies in overcoming this frustration...*
>
> *We've been able to help our clients overcome this challenge...*
>
> *We've helped our clients eliminate this obstacle...*

Bold value statements don't have to be long or elaborate. Their purpose is to add power to the call. You not only want to project confidence, you want to grab the attention of the buyer with a statement that implies value.

Step 4: State the Purpose of Your Call

Stating the purpose of your call acts as a transitional phrase, bringing the power benefit statement to a close and serving as a springboard to either qualify the account or set an appointment.

As a member of a local central committee of a national political party, I received a call from an aspiring politician who spoke to me for close to an hour about issues, resolutions, and pending legislation. I finally cut him off and said, "What is it you want from me?" Because of my radio show and clout with some of the local and state party members, he wanted me to endorse some of his ideas, but it had taken him an hour to get to the purpose of his call. By then I was frustrated from listening to him and was looking for an opportunity to get off the phone. Had he called me and said, "Patrick, I'm concerned about the following issues and want your support to do something about it," I would have had a much more positive response.

> **Caution!** Avoid being vague when stating the purpose of your call. Ambiguous, imprecise statements cause frustration and confusion instead of clarity.

Buyers find it frustrating when they can't decipher what the point or purpose of a business conversation is. When stating the purpose for your call, you should be exact; there is no reason to be timid or shy when making a cold call. If you are attempting to set up an appointment and you verbally fumble around instead of offering an exact date and time, you lose momentum. So, be specific. Say to the buyer, "Are you available to meet next Tuesday morning at 9:00?" Be clear, precise, and to the point. It's far more compelling to offer a client an exact date and time than saying, "What I would like to do is set up a time when we can meet." How can potential clients say, "Yes" to that? They can't.

I consulted with a company that sells specialized pain relief mattress layovers. They use a patented product called Intelligel to provide customers with the latest in cushion technology. We put together numerous cold call scripts and tested each of them in a targeted market in order to set up appointments. We created some terrific cold calling scripts... that didn't work. We tested numerous versions of the same script with little to no improvement, so we finally decided that we would state the reason for our call early in the script and offer an exact date and time for an appointment. It worked beautifully, and we actually exceeded our prospecting expectations! The key to success was providing a clear reason for calling and offering a precise date and time to meet.

> **The Point?** If the purpose of your call is to set an appointment, it's important to offer an exact date and time. Make it easy for the prospect to say, "Yes." Don't beat around the bush. If an appointment is what you want, ask for it.

Sample Purpose Statements

"Hi Ms. Jones, this is Brian Jennings with *Patrick Henry & Associates*. We've recently been working with pharmaceutical companies in the areas of cold calling and sales training, most recently at ABC Company. A consistent problem I'm hearing from other executives is the difficulty their sales reps experience trying to fill their pipelines with qualified accounts. We've developed an effective strategy to help our clients overcome this frustration."

> *And I would like to set up an appointment to discuss ways in which we might be able to do the same thing for you. Are you available to meet next Tuesday morning at 9:00?*

"One of the problems we consistently encounter when talking to other executives is their disappointment over the inability of their sales reps to negotiate profitable agreements."

> *The reason I'm calling today is simply to set up an appointment to discuss with you how we've been able to help our clients overcome this challenge. Are you available to meet next Tuesday at 9:00?*

> *I'd like to stop by next Tuesday at 9:00 and share with you the success we recently experienced with ABC Company.*

Many sellers feel more comfortable offering buyers optional dates and times to meet, so rather than offering a single date and time, they offer optional dates and times (referred to as the dual date and time tactic). Using this tactic, a salesperson would conclude the opening statement by saying, "Are you available Tuesday at 9:00 or Thursday at 2:00?" The rationale behind the dual date and time technique is simple. By providing optional dates and times to meet, buyers think in terms of when to meet, not whether to meet.

> **Caution!** The dual date and time tactic is a popular prospecting technique, and that's the problem. It's used so frequently that many buyers recognize it as an overused, manipulative sales tactic rather than a professional sales approach.

Sellers engaged in appointment-based cold calls should consider offering off-hour meeting times. Instead of offering to meet at 9:00 A.M., a typical meeting hour, a seller might offer to meet at 9:20 A.M. The reasoning behind this tactic is two-fold: first, it conveys to buyers that your time is valuable, and second, it communicates to buyers that you are punctual.

If you are engaged in qualification-based cold calls (versus appointment-based cold calls) and are not certain whether or not it is worth your time to meet with the potential client, i.e., they may not be qualified to purchase your product or service, do not mention a time to meet. Simply conclude the power benefit statement without mentioning an appointment. For example,

> "Hi, this is Savannah with Acme Software. We've recently been working with I.T. executives for large banks. A common concern they share with us is the lack of technical integration between different departments within their organization. We've helped our clients solve this problem with enterprise-wide software and networking solutions and would welcome an opportunity to discuss with you how we might be able to resolve similar dilemmas you might be experiencing."

By concluding the benefit statement without mentioning a time to meet, it signals to the buyer that you are anticipating a conversation. It also ends in a way that makes a yes/no response difficult.

If you are following up on a personal letter or direct mail campaign, step four of the power benefit statement is also a good time to reference a previous point of contact. Mention the letter as part of the reason for your call:

> "Hi Ms. Jones, this is Gloria Simpson with *Patrick Henry & Associates.* We've recently been working with manufacturing companies in the areas of sales and negotiation training, most recently at ABC Company. One of the primary concerns I'm hearing from other executives is the difficulty many of their sales reps have selling without discounting. *The reason I am calling is because I recently sent you information regarding how Patrick Henry & Associates has helped our clients overcome this challenge,* and I would like an opportunity to share with you how we might be able to do the same thing for you."

Step 5: Listen

Listening is the last step of the power benefit statement. (The importance of listening is discussed in Chapter 12). After completing the opening statement, be quiet and let the buyer talk without interrupting. If he or she agrees to an appointment, say, "Thank you," confirm the date and time, and move on. Avoid a premature presentation on the phone or "spilling your candy in the lobby" by saying too much too soon.

One of the most difficult tasks for sellers is to know when to be silent. Sellers are often tempted to keep talking at the conclusion of the benefit statement, especially if the buyer is silent. *You must avoid this temptation.* Even if the buyer is silent, wait until he or she responds.

Many sellers are poor listeners. Far too many salespeople believe they need to immediately immerse the buyer in information about their product or service. This is a costly mistake that should be avoided, especially on the first call.

> **The Point?** Once *The Power Benefit Statement* is completed, *listen*. Take notes and focus on discovery-qualification questions. (See Chapter 10).

Completed Power Benefit Statements

The following benefit statements are cold call scripts used by *Patrick Henry & Associates* to generate qualified accounts and set up appointments.

> "Good morning Mr. Smith, this is Derris Moore with *Patrick Henry & Associates* calling from New York City. We provide sales and presentation training for medical device manufacturers. Some of our clients include ABC Corporation and XYZ Manufacturer. One of the primary concerns we are hearing from other executives is their frustration with ineffective sales presentations. The reason I'm calling today is simply to set up an appointment to discuss with you how we've been able to help our clients overcome this challenge and deliver exceptional presentations. Are you available to meet next Tuesday morning at 9:20?"

> "Good afternoon Ms. Jones, my name is Holly Layne. I'm an account executive for *Patrick Henry & Associates*. We've recently been working with the technical industry in the areas of sales and negotiation training. A consistent problem we are hearing from sales managers is the difficulty many of their salespeople experience negotiating. We've been able to help our clients overcome this challenge and negotiate more profitable agreements. The purpose of my call is simply to set up an appointment to discuss ways in which we might be able to do the same thing for you. Are you available to meet next Tuesday morning at 9:20?"

> "Hi Alan, this is Zac Fenton with *Patrick Henry & Associates*. We've recently been working with mortgage companies in the

areas of cold calling and sales training. A consistent concern we hear from other executives is their frustration with loan officers who struggle to close qualified accounts. The reason I'm calling today is because we just completed working with ABC Company and were successful in helping their loan officers increase their close ratios by over 30 percent. What I would like to do is discuss with you how we might be able to provide your business with similar results."

> **Note:** I do not recommend the previous scripts be used verbatim. Instead, I recommend using our basic structure and implementing the principles we've reviewed to create a prospecting script that works for you.

Because it will need work and modification as you refine your approach, don't expect your script or delivery to be perfect the first time. Cold calling is a science. Like all other sciences, practice and experiment until you find what script or method works best for you.

The Power Benefit Statement

Figure 10.2

Create a Power Benefit Statement

There is a significant difference between a "canned" and a "planned" sales call. By creating and rehearsing sales scripts, prospecting calls become second nature. Sales professionals who create a power benefit statement in the form of a script are more confident and more productive. Use the following framework to create your own power benefit statement.

1. Introduce and identify yourself, your company, and (optional) your location:

2. State a common reference:

3. Make a bold value statement:

4. State the purpose of your call:

5. Listen

> **Caution!** Prospecting calls must sound conversational to be effective. Calls cannot sound as though they are being read from a script. Once you have created a script, rehearse and master its content to "conversationalize" it.

CHAPTER 11

The DNASelling Method

On February 28, 1953, Francis Crick walked into the Eagle pub in Cambridge, England, and announced that he and James Watson had "found the secret of life." In just a few weeks of frenzied inspiration, the two men made one of the most profound discoveries in history by building a model of deoxyribonucleic acid (DNA) that demonstrated how the very structure of DNA provides one of life's most essential features: the storage and transmission of genetic code. The men had solved a problem that had been baffling the scientific community for years—how did the DNA molecule make exact copies of itself? Biochemists already knew that DNA contained a biological code, a genetic language that consists of four types of molecules, known as bases—adenine, cytosine, thymine, and guanine—referred to as A, C, G, and T, but how those molecules made exact replicas of each other was still a mystery.

Back in the Cavendish Laboratory in Cambridge, Watson and Crick concentrated on identifying the *form* of DNA rather than its *function*. They built model after model of the possible structure of DNA until on March 7, 1953, they discovered the solution: DNA is a double helix shaped like a spiral staircase with the four bases representing the steps. Their model suggested a mechanism by which DNA could make copies of itself. The two strands of genes that made up the DNA molecule can simply unzip or unravel into reverse images of each other that can act as templates for new strands to build on.

The genius of DNA is that *its form is its function*. Its shockingly simplistic double helix structure allows the molecules to make facsimiles of itself, and because the bases always bond in the exact sequence, the finished copies are always the same. The concept was stunning in its implications.

Using the scientific method, Watson and Crick made the most

celebrated discovery of the twentieth century. The double helix

now stands as an icon of the scientific understanding of life.

——➤●◄——

The Science of Selling

Like most sales professionals, I learned early in my career that selling
was more of a science than an art. I learned that asking the right questions was more important than looking for the right answers; however,
knowing the importance of asking the right questions was not enough.
My questions seemed random and, at times, even uncomfortable.
Asking questions "off the top of my head" was sporadic and ineffective.
This unorganized approach quite often left me tongue-tied and unable
to communicate effectively. I needed a system—a questioning methodology. I needed a process that was easy to understand, easy to remember, and easy to replicate from one sale to the next. I decided to write
down a series of questions that I deemed important to making sales, I
then organized the questions into categories. For example, I separated
qualification questions from questions that identified client needs. I
differentiated need related questions from solution related questions.
The result was *The DNASelling Method*—a questioning methodology
that leads buyers through the sales cycle.

The Same Way DNA Consists of the Building Blocks of Life, *The DNASelling Method* Consists of the Building Blocks of Effective Selling

Similar in concept to DNA, *The DNASelling Method* is a selling language—a code of questions that sales professionals ask buyers. It is
a process of discovery—a questioning framework whose "form is its
function."

The DNASelling Method is a question-based approach to selling
that follows a rational probing sequence and provides sellers with a
systematic approach to qualifying accounts and closing sales. Like the
four bases of DNA, *The DNASelling Method* consists of four probing

categories that guide buyers and sellers through the purchasing process.

> **Discovery-Qualification Questions**: Questions that discover a buyer's existing circumstance, account facts, qualification factors, and purchasing capabilities.

> **Need-Problem Questions**: Questions that identify a buyer's needs, problems, and primary buying motives.

> **Ascertain-Pain Questions**: Questions that ascertain the negative consequences of unfulfilled needs and/or unresolved problems, i.e., the pain.

> **Solution-Benefit Questions**: Questions that focus on the benefits of implementing the proposed solution.

Because questioning is such a fundamental part of successful selling, it's important to use an effective questioning methodology—a strategy. By using *The DNASelling Method*, sellers add structure, repeatability, and predictability to the questioning and selling process.

> **Note:** *The DNASelling Method* is a holistic questioning approach. For prospecting purposes, only the first two steps of *The DNASelling Method* are emphasized in this book.

Discovery-Qualification Questions

The first stage of the sales cycle is the prospecting stage. In the prospecting stage, sellers focus on asking questions, acquiring account information, and qualifying accounts. By using discovery-qualification questions sellers equip themselves with the information they need to progress the prospecting call into a sales call.

Discovery-qualification questions are primarily used in qualification-based cold calls. As discussed in Chapter 6, qualification-based

The DNASelling Method

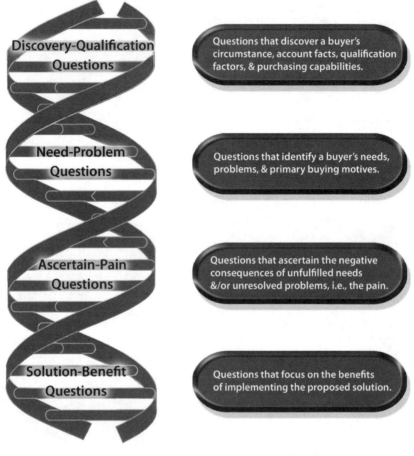

Discovery-Qualification Questions

Questions that discover a buyer's circumstance, account facts, qualification factors, & purchasing capabilities.

Need-Problem Questions

Questions that identify a buyer's needs, problems, & primary buying motives.

Ascertain-Pain Questions

Questions that ascertain the negative consequences of unfulfilled needs &/or unresolved problems, i.e., the pain.

Solution-Benefit Questions

Questions that focus on the benefits of implementing the proposed solution.

Figure 11.1

cold calls move sellers from the prospecting stage of the sales cycle to the investigation stage of the sales cycle—in a single call. The remaining steps of *The DNASelling Method* rely on information gained from discovery-qualification questions.

Discovering Account Facts

A wise man doesn't give the right answers, he poses the right questions.

—Claude Levi-Strauss

In his waning years, Prussian premier Otto von Bismarck developed cancer. His wife, Johanna, brought in a new, young doctor to attend him. At their first meeting the chancellor told him brusquely, "I don't like questions." "Then get a veterinarian," replied the doctor. "They don't question their patients."

Good doctors do not initially worry about getting the right answers. They concentrate on asking the right questions. They make intelligent inquiries, take notes, make observations, and listen intently. They gather information instead of providing it.

The most brilliant thinkers, innovators, and explorers of our time emphasized questions more than answers, a characteristic of highly intelligent individuals. Note the root of the word question is "quest"— the act of seeking or pursuing something, a search beyond that which is already known.

Discovery questions are probes that focus on a prospect's existing circumstance and discover account facts, background information, and fundamental issues related to the sale. For example, a salesperson selling vehicles would ask discovery questions such as, "Mr. Jones, are you looking for trucks or vans for your delivery business?" "Are your current delivery vehicles two or four wheel drive?" A salesperson selling networking solutions would ask discovery questions to determine what networking platform the prospect is using. "Ms. Prospect, what platform are you currently using, Microsoft or Novell?" "What version of Novell are you using to run your servers?" etc. Discovery questions not only reveal insightful information, sometimes they expose certain biases prospects have. For example, a simple discovery question might reveal that a prospect is a Novell fanatic and hates Microsoft networking solutions.

I managed a salesperson who continually neglected to ask simple discovery questions. He seemed to view them as a waste of time and instead preferred to jump to the presentation stage of the sales cycle. He once made a sale that illustrates the importance of asking discovery questions.

A few weeks after selling a complete software and networking solution to a client in British Columbia, the technical administrator who made the purchase called to inform me that he was returning our software. I was stunned as this was a big sale, and I was totally unaware of any problems or mishaps. I asked the buyer why he wanted to return our product. He told me that he felt that our salespeople were dishonest and that he did not want to deal with a company that took advantage of their customers. When I asked him why he felt that way, he stated, "Because your sales rep sold us a Web-based product knowing that we did not yet have the hardware or networking infrastructure in place to use it!"

When I approached our salesperson to find out what happened, he was shocked to find out that they did not have the hardware or networking capability to use our Web client. He just assumed they had the technical requirements to implement our Web-based line of products. Because he failed to ask simple discovery questions that would have identified their exact technical capabilities, he sold them a solution they couldn't use.

> **The Point?** Equipped with information that identifies a buyer's existing circumstance and account facts, sellers make better recommendations, deliver account-specific presentations, and close more sales.

Question Rationale

In 1582, Protestants in the Netherlands were struggling to gain independence from their Catholic overseer, Spain. Brutal executions and cruel torturing techniques rallied the Dutch Protestants to revolt. Seeking assistance from England, the

Protestant rebels appealed to Queen Elizabeth I. Not wishing to engage in open warfare with Spain, the most powerful empire in the world, Elizabeth resisted intervention. By 1585, however, she assented to a treaty which bound her to send an army to assist the Dutch Protestants. Before committing English troops, however, she issued an extraordinary twenty-page pamphlet, translated it into French, Spanish, and Dutch, and distributed it across England and the European Continent. This pamphlet was an unprecedented move—a sovereign ruler justifying her actions before the opinions of the world. In her political treatise, she provided the reason and rationale for her intervention. She discussed the tyrannical nature of Spanish governors and outlined the violation of "ancient laws of liberty." The pamphlet had the desired effect and rallied Protestants across Europe to support her decision.

Although salespeople should never feel obliged to apologize for their questions, like Queen Elizabeth I, they should be prepared to provide rationale to justify their inquiries.

Remember when you were a kid how much you feared your neighbors' big dog? When you hit a ball over the fence and had to retrieve it, how did you speak to the dog? More than likely you approached the dog saying, "Nice doggy. Easy boy. Good dog." Why? You didn't want your language or tone to arouse the hostility of the dog. Rationale statements do the same thing. They remove the potential harshness of the question or approach.

Prospects should not feel like they are being grilled with unnecessary, useless, or endless questions, so "tee up" your questions with a statement of rationale. The statement of rationale softens the probe and justifies the question.

For each questioning category in *The DNASelling Method*, a statement of rationale is provided prior to the sample question.

Sample Discovery Questions

Rationale: "Mr. Prospect, I would like to tell you about [name of your product or service]; however, in order for me to do the best job I possibly can for you, I need to ask you a few questions about how you are currently [managing X]."

- Tell me more about _____.
- What are you using at present to _____?
- Help me understand how you currently _____.
- Tell me a little bit about _____.
- How many _____.
- How long have you been using _____?
- Tell me how you presently_____.
- How many people utilize _____?

Qualifying Sales Opportunities

In respect of military method, we have, firstly Measurements; secondly, Estimation of Quantity; thirdly, Calculation; fourthly, Balancing of Chances; fifthly, Victory.

–Sun-Tzu

George Armstrong Custer fought in the Civil War at the first battle of Bull Run. He distinguished himself as a member of General McClellan's staff in the Peninsular campaign, and was made a brigadier general of volunteers in June, 1863. The youngest general in the Union army, Custer ably led a cavalry brigade in the Gettysburg campaign and was made a divisional commander in October, 1864. During the spring of 1865 Custer was in hot pursuit against Lee's army in Richmond, Virginia. In April, 1865, Custer received the Confederate flag of truce and was present when

General Lee surrendered at the Appomattox Courthouse. His military record, considering his youth, was one of the most spectacular of the Civil War.

In the reorganization of the U.S. army after the war Custer was assigned to the 7th Cavalry. In 1875 his regiment was deployed to fight in the Indian conflicts in the west. President Grant, who had a low opinion of the Indians, ordered the Lakotas and neighboring tribes to leave the Great Plains, where they were in conflict with the ranches. This, following the systematic destruction of buffalo, led to the Great Sioux War of 1876.

In the campaign against the Sioux, Custer, now a member of the 7th Cavalry, was sent forward to locate the enemy. Custer came upon a combined Sioux-Cheyenne encampment near the valley of the Little Bighorn River on June 25 and decided to attack at once. Without conducting pre-battle reconnaissance or determining the size and fighting capability of Crazy Horse and his warriors, Custer ordered an immediate attack. Not realizing the overwhelming numerical superiority of the Indians, most of whom lay concealed in ravines, he divided his regiment into three parts, sending two of them, under Major Marcus A. Reno and Capt. Frederick W. Benteen, to attack farther upstream, while he himself led the third (over 200 men) in a direct charge. Every one of them was killed in battle. The men (except Custer, whose remains were reinterred at West Point) were buried on the battlefield, now a national monument in Montana. "Custer's Last Stand," daring charge and spectacular death made him a popular but controversial American hero.

The mistake Custer made was rushing into battle without exploring the terrain, scouting his enemy, or determining the probable success of a frontal attack. Had Custer conducted even a modicum of reconnaissance, he would have discovered that his planned assault would lead to the annihilation of his entire regiment.

Similar to General Custer's famous but disastrous attack at the battle of Little Bighorn, many salespeople charge into sales without surveying the situation, conducting adequate account reconnaissance, or determining win capability.

Picking winnable battles is a trademark of successful sellers. Even sellers with polished communication skills, incredible product knowledge, and powerful personalities cannot be successful unless they concentrate on prospects with the greatest purchasing potential.

Has this ever happened to you? You contact a prospect, gain his or her attention, present your product, answer questions, and prepare a proposal. You send a follow up letter, leave messages, and finally talk to the prospect about a few specific issues, but when you call back a week later, he or she tells you, "Your presentation was excellent, but I talked to my boss and he just isn't interested."

What happened? What went wrong?

Obviously, the account was not properly qualified. Had the account been qualified, the ultimate decision maker (the boss) would have attended the presentation.

Sales success depends on a seller's ability to qualify leads and gain account information critical to winning a sale *prior to investing TIME (Time, Investment, Money & Effort) into the sale.* There are many interested people who will never buy. The level of buyer interest is meaningless without the ability or willingness to purchase the proposed good or service. This is why qualifying is so critical to successful selling—it helps sellers make better time, investment decisions, and avoid dealing with "strokers and jokers," "fence sitters," and "tire kickers."

Qualification Characteristics

The DNASelling Method provides sellers with an organized procedure to analyze each selling opportunity systematically. Because many salespeople make the mistake of pursuing every prospect with the same tenacity, it is important to use a proven system of opportunity eval-

> **Note:** Qualifying is the most important step in *The DNASelling Method*.

uation. By implementing *The DNASelling Method*, sellers follow an objective, diligent qualification process that allows them to allocate their time more efficiently and deal with accounts that have the highest probability for success.

While selling educational software, I received a call from a prospect interested in our product. The prospect asked me to fill out a lengthy RFP (request for proposal). I invested a considerable amount of time filling out the RFP. After it was completed, I submitted the RFP to my contact person and casually asked, "So what's the timeframe on this project?" She replied, "Well, we are hoping to get a grant from the government in early spring." My heart sank as I realized what had just happened. This prospect used me to gain information to assist his efforts to acquire a government grant that would then *possibly* be used to purchase my product. I could not believe I had been so stupid. That experience burned a permanent reminder in my mind to never, ever invest TIME (Time, Investment, Money & Effort) on a prospect who is not thoroughly qualified.

As mentioned in Chapter 6, a qualified prospect in any industry has four general characteristics:

1. Ultimate Decision-maker(s)
2. Available Funding
3. Acceptable Timeframe(s)
4. Matching Needs

If any one of the qualifying components is missing, the probability of closing the sale is diminished. By asking simple qualification questions, sellers identify all four qualifying characteristics and enhance the probability of working with clients who are likely to purchase.

Because some leads are temptations disguised as opportunities, it's important to use a systematic approach to qualify contacts. Without a consistent process for qualifying buyers, sellers lose valuable time they might otherwise have used to pursue genuine opportunities.

Qualifying (or disqualifying) prevents sellers from wasting time. Remember, the objective of selling is to spend time with prospects who need, want, and *can* purchase products and services.

> **The Point?** You can't sell to someone who can't buy, so be sure to qualify accounts before investing significant amounts of TIME into a sale.

Creating Question Sheets

When I first started my sales career, I learned that relying solely on memory to come up with good qualifying questions was naïve, so I created "question sheets" to assist me in asking good questions. I would print the question sheets, put them in paper protectors, place them on my desk, and reference them during my calls. It was extremely effective since it systematized my qualifying efforts. It was also the beginning of *The DNASelling Method.*

By creating question sheets, I essentially built a library of questions to reference during the investigation stage of the selling process. The following sample qualification questions are taken from those initial sheets.

Sample *Decision—Maker* Qualification Questions

Rationale: "Mr. Prospect, based on our experience in the X market, there are usually many people involved in making purchasing decisions."

- Who, other than yourself, will be involved in making the final decision?
- A system like _____ usually affects people at several levels of an organization. Who else is involved in the decision making process?
- Is there anyone else you usually consult with when making decisions of this type?
- Aside from yourself, who will be involved in the decision making process?
- Is there anyone else who needs to be involved in order to make a decision?

> **Caution!** Do not ask questions that insinuate the person you are speaking with is not a decision-maker.

Remember, not everyone can make a decision, but many people can pull the plug on your opportunity to sell. The bulk of your time should be spent with people who can put decision ink on paper, so be sure to deal with decision makers.

Sample *Funding* Qualification Questions

Rationale: "Ms. Prospect, implementation of a project like this usually depends on available funding."

- How do you normally fund a project like this?
- If you did choose to _____, is funding available to implement?
- [ABC Product] can cost anywhere between X and Y dollars depending on what you want to accomplish. How are you planning to fund this project?
- Depending on your specific needs, [automated systems] range between X and Y dollars. What does your budget look like for this project?
- This particular model requires an initial investment of X dollars, and a monthly investment of Y. Is that an acceptable investment range?
- What kind of a budget are you working with?
- Assuming there is a fit between the problems you are experiencing and what I'm offering, the investment is going to run between X and Y dollars. Has funding been allocated for this project?

An additional advantage for asking funding related questions is preventing finances from becoming a barrier later in the selling process. By dealing with the money issues up front, you defuse the "we can't afford it" objection before it turns up.

Sample *Timeframe* Qualification Questions

Rationale: "Mr. Prospect, implementation of a project like this usually depends on available funding. What sort of timeframe are you working

> **Note:** Used appropriately, the sample timeframe rationale question will answer both funding and timeframe issues.

- Are you working with any decision deadlines?
- How is the purchase decision being made?
- How soon do you plan on making a decision?
- As you look at implementing a _____, what kind of timeframe are you working with?
- Will it be possible for you to purchase in the present budget cycle?
- What decision making process do you go through when deciding on a purchase such as this?
- When do you see yourself moving forward with this project?
- If you decided to go forward, when would you want to start?
- Thank you for telling me the timeframe. How does the decision timeframe relate to the implementation date?

Cerebral sellers match time and effort with appropriate buying cycles and implementation dates, discover real timeframes, and adjust their selling efforts accordingly.

Matching Needs

The final qualifying factor in any sale is matching needs. In order for a lead to be considered qualified, product or service capabilities must match client needs. Problems, pains, and dissatisfactions need to correspond to potential product offerings and service solutions. (For a detailed analysis of matching needs, and to review sample need-problem questions, see Chapter 12).

When to Qualify Leads

Although qualifying sales opportunities is important, sellers should not get stymied trying to qualify the account in the first few minutes of the initial sales call.

I traveled to Cancun, Mexico to conduct sales training for a group of salespeople at their annual corporate retreat. Part of the training focused on qualifying accounts, and as part of our ongoing coaching program, I worked with a very intense salesperson who seemed to understand the letter of the law but failed to understand the spirit of the law. He implemented our training on qualification and began qualifying accounts, but there was just one problem. He qualified his accounts in the immediate moments of his sales calls. Because dealing with people who could not purchase his product just did not make sense to him, he decided to immediately qualify his leads, and it didn't work. He didn't warm up his calls with friendly conversation. He failed to put buyers at ease. When he neglected to discover account information and just jumped right into qualifying the candidate, it backfired because people felt like they were getting bashed with questions. He became an overzealous seller rather than a cerebral seller.

Implementing *The DNASelling Method*

Training graduates frequently ask, "How am I going to remember to ask all of these questions?" The answer is, of course, "You're not." The sample questions are simply *lists* of *potential* questions to choose from.

To implement *The DNASelling Method*, sellers need to select a few questions from each category, write them down, and memorize them before adapting them to individual situations. As our training graduates have proven over and over again, with a little bit of time and effort, the questions become second nature in sales conversations.

Note: It is not necessary to memorize dozens of sales related questions. Instead, memorize two or three questions from each category of *The DNASelling Method* that you feel most comfortable with.

In Summary

The DNASelling Method is a logical and orderly approach to selling. It is a system that has been validated in a wide variety of markets, industries, and cultures. It works. It is a sequential, step-by-step process that mirrors the sales cycle and guides prospects through the buying process.

The reason the *The DNASelling Method* is so effective is that it provides sellers with a system to qualify accounts and ask intelligent, insightful questions. When sellers do not systematize their questions, they are not as successful. When sellers fail to use a clear and simple model for asking prospects questions, they stumble through the selling process.

Using *The DNASelling Method* gives sellers an edge over competitors. When sellers commit to making *The DNASelling Method* part of their selling strategy, they stand out from the thousands of salespeople who sell on instinct instead of intellect.

The Point? Successful sellers recognize that larger sales are a compilation of small sales. By following *The DNASelling Method*, sellers experience a series of small successes early in the sales relationship that eventually lead to the final sale.

CHAPTER 12

Need-Problem Questions

———————

Genghis Khan was one of the most barbaric and brutal leaders in history. His conquests in China in the twelfth century were fierce and merciless, and he threatened to destroy a culture that had thrived for close to two thousand years. Uncultured himself, Khan saw no value in Chinese art, literature, architecture, or culture and cared about nothing more than the practical results of battle. Nomadic by nature, Khan saw China as a land with little pasture and not enough grass to feed his primary weapon of warfare, horses.

On the verge of devastating China, Khan appointed an advisor, Ch'u-Ts'ai, who recognized the value of the Chinese culture and secretly worked to protect it. A foreigner himself, Ch'u-Ts'ai had come to appreciate the superiority of the Chinese culture and attempted to prevent Khan from totally destroying it.

When Khan's army was about to annihilate a major Chinese city, Ch'u-Ts'ai stepped in and convinced Khan that it would be more beneficial to tax the inhabitants than to destroy them, and Khan agreed. When Khan's armies conquered the Chinese city of Kaifeng, Khan ordered the massacre of its inhabitants, as he had done to all of the cities that resisted him. But Ch'u-Ts'ai convinced Khan that the finest engineers and craftsmen in China were from Kaifeng and that they would be of great value to him, so Khan agreed and spared the citizens of Kaifeng.

Ch'u-Ts'ai continued his clandestine efforts to save the Chinese people and their culture. He did so by appealing to the most powerful force known to man—self-interest. By appealing to the needs, interests, and desires of a cruel dictator, Ch'u-Ts'ai was able to prevent the total destruction of the Chinese people and their culture.

Self-interest is the catalyst that moves people to act. When people see how you can meet their needs, eliminate their problems, or advance their interests, they will readily agree to recommendations and proposals. This is why cerebral sellers appeal to the needs, issues, and primary buying motives of buyers and focus on the interests of prospects. They identify what is important to clients and use the power of self-interest to their advantage.

Using Need-Problem Questions in the Initial Sales Call

If you can learn a simple trick, you'll get along a lot better with all kinds of folks. You never really understand a person until you consider things from his point of view... until you climb into his skin and walk around in it.

—Atticus Finch to his daughter, Scout,
in *To Kill a Mockingbird*

The second stage of the sales cycle is the investigation stage. In the investigation stage sellers gather information, identify needs, and determine prospective problems to match to product or service solutions. Need-problem questions transition calls from the prospecting stage of the sales cycle to the investigation stage of the sales cycle.

Like a verbal detective, the tools of the trade for cerebral sellers are questions. Questions demonstrate concern for a prospect's needs and place the focus of the sales process where it belongs: on the prospect. As the great sales educator Zig Ziglar stated, sellers should always "Lead with need." Unfortunately, most salespeople instinctively jump from prospecting to presenting and miss the most vital step in the selling process, investigating.

No selling skill has more of an impact on the success or failure of a sale than the ability of a seller to identify a prospective buyer's needs, problems, and pains. That bears repeating. *Nothing you do in the selling process is more important than discovering needs, identifying problems, and determining the primary buying motives of buyers.*

Note: A needs analysis is much more than just a discovery process. The competitive battle is often won in the investigation stage of the sales cycle *before* the sales presentation even takes place.

Review *The DNASelling Method*:

- Discovery-Qualification Questions
- Need-Problem Questions
- Ascertain-Pain Questions
- Solution-Benefit Questions

The second step of *The DNASelling Method* is asking need-problem questions. Need-problem questions dig for "buzz issues," "hot buttons," and identify subjects that can be used to create high impact presentations and fuel the sales process.

With need-related information, sales professionals equip themselves with the required data to make account specific, credible recommendations. *Without* need-related information, sales professionals cannot "sell to needs." And without needs to fill or problems to solve, there is probably little basis for a sale in the first place.

Need-Problem questions form the foundation of a successful sale and supply sellers with three essential benefits:

1. Determining if there is a "good fit" between problems and solutions
2. Identifying the buyer's primary buying motives
3. Building credibility and rapport with buyers

Results are precise and accurate recommendations that buyers take seriously. Sellers who unearth buyer needs and problems and then incorporate them into sales presentations become respected consultants instead of product pushers. As Stephen R. Covey says, "When you can present your own ideas clearly, specifically, visually, and most important, contextually—in the context of a deep understanding of [a

buyer's] paradigms and concerns—you significantly increase the credibility of your idea... You're not wrapped up in your 'own thing,' delivering grandiose rhetoric from a soapbox."[1]

My neighbor shared with me a story that illustrates the importance
of asking need-problem questions. Years ago his parents lived in the
foothills of the Wasatch Mountains in Utah, and during the winter the
snow was so deep that they needed a snow blower to remove the snow
from their driveway. When their snow blower broke, his father went to
a local hardware store to buy a new one. As he was evaluating the snow
blowers on display, a salesperson approached him and said, "We've got
a terrific sale on this model right here (pointing to a particular snow
blower)." His father bought the snow blower and later told his son,
"I was prepared to spend up to $5,000 on a heavy duty snow blower.
Instead, I bought the one on sale for $799."

The hardware store salesman sold a $799 product to a buyer who
was willing to spend up to $5,000 on a high quality snow blower,
leaving money on the table because he failed to ask a few simple need
related questions. Had he simply asked, "Mr. Buyer, what kind of a
snow blower are you looking for?" or, "How much snow do you normally have to remove?" he could have recommended a snow blower
that matched the needs and wants of the buyer, rather than making
a recommendation based on a sales price or spiff. Had the hardware
salesman asked the buyer questions about the depth of snow, the slope
of their driveway, or whether or not his wife would also be operating the snow blower, he could have confirmed the need to purchase a
higher quality, more heavy-duty snow blower. He lost commissionable
dollars and failed to fully meet the needs of his customer because he
neglected to ask need-related questions.

A shopper searching for kitchen knives in the house wares department of a retail store asked a salesperson "Are these kitchen knives
sharp?" The salesperson answered, "Oh yes. They have been honed
with laser technology. They cut deeply, leaving no rough edge." The

---

1. Stephen R. Covey, *The 7 Habits of Highly Effective People* (New York: Simon
and Schuster, 1989) 257.

shopper replied, "Oh. My mother loves to cook but has arthritis. I'd be afraid she would get a nasty cut."

The intent of the shopper's question was not to gain information about the technology of the knives. The intent was to introduce the issue of safety. Before rushing in with an answer a cerebral salesperson would have responded with a need related question, "Are sharp knives important to you?"

Need-problem questions help sales professionals sell with greater accuracy and greater integrity. Equipped with information about the needs, problems, difficulties, and dissatisfactions of buyers, sellers are better prepared to make substantive recommendations, deliver meaningful presentations, and become respected consultants rather than biased product pushers.

There is another benefit of using need-problem questions. The *process* of identifying needs has a positive affect on the psyche of buyers. When sellers provide buyers with an opportunity to participate in defining the problems, buyers develop a sense of ownership in the sale. When buyers help define the problem, they are more easily persuaded to purchase the solution.

The Point? No problem = no sale. Needs and problems are to a sale what oxygen is to a fire. People only buy if they have needs to fill or problems to resolve.

Sample Need-Problem Questions

Rationale: "Mr. Prospect, as a [business] consultant for [*Patrick Henry & Associates*], it's my job to understand and analyze any current needs you face with regard to [sales performance] and then do my best to come up with solutions to address those problems."

Sample Need Questions

- As you look at this project, what are your most critical needs?
- What's the most significant issue you currently face?
- What is it you're looking for in a _____?
- As you look at _____, what capabilities are most critical to you?
- What would you like to accomplish with _____?
- What benefits are you most interested in when evaluating _____?
- What is the most important factor for you in making this decision?
- What else would help me understand _____?
- What would help you do your job better?
- What are three things you would like to see improved?

Sample Problem Questions

- What are the most important problems you would like to resolve?
- What problems are you currently experiencing?
- What are the most critical challenges you currently face?
- Help me understand what area is giving you the most problems.
- What created these problems?
- What problems do you face with your current _____?
- Are you experiencing any dissatisfaction with _____?
- What is the cause of the problem you are experiencing _____?
- What does it currently take to manage _____?
- Is there anything about your current situation you don't like?
- Where do you see a need for improvement?
- If you could invent a product or service to solve your problems, what would it do?

Of course, the point is not to ask endless questions or gather infinite information. Each question should clarify the prospect's needs and problems so that informed proposals, customized presentations, and accurate recommendations can be made. (To assist sellers implement *The DNASelling Method*, a sample DNASelling Call Sheet has been included at the end of this chapter to help sellers plan and execute call strategies, and focus on the critical components of a sales call).

Question Types

What was God doing before he created heaven and earth? He was preparing hell for people who ask awkward questions.

—St. Augustine

There are three general types of sales questions:

1. *Yes-No Questions:* Yes-No questions can only be answered with a "Yes" or a "No" and are sometimes called clarifying or fact finding questions. For example, "Are you insured?"

2. *Closed-Ended Questions*: Closed-ended questions result in single word answers. They are sometimes called confirming or targeted questions. For example, "Is it an individual or group policy?"

3. *Open-Ended Questions*: Open-ended questions usually result in multi worded answers and are sometimes called exploratory or thought provoking questions. For example, "Why did you choose policy X?"

Using Closed-ended Questions in the Initial Sales Call

Closed-ended questions have become a dirty word in the selling industry. Many sales and marketing courses teach that closed-ended questions have no place in a salesperson's vernacular. However, nothing could be further from the truth. Instructing sellers to never use closed-ended questions is "throwing the baby out with the bath water" because each question type has its appropriate time and place.

That is not to say that in certain situations one question type is not better than another. When you are seeking quantitative (quantity related) information, open-ended questions provide precise information; whereas, when you are seeking qualitative (clear and definitive) information, closed-ended and yes-no questions are more effective.

Yes-No (and most closed-ended questions) generally start with the phrases:

Can you _____?
Do you _____?
Have you _____?
Does it _____?
Is it _____?
Are you _____?
Has it _____?

In the initial stages of the sale, closed-ended questions are appropriate because they solicit clear and definitive answers.

> **Note:** Don't be afraid to use closed-ended questions early in the sales call to obtain specific account information.

Open Ended Questions

Although closed-ended questions are effective sales tools, they should not be over used. Closed-ended questions are excellent tools for obtaining clear and definitive information, but are not particularly effective for building long-term relationships.

Open-ended questions are less direct, more conversational, and solicit more information from buyers. Open-ended questions overcome the "clam" effect by encouraging buyers to offer information that can be used to advance the sale.

Open-ended questions are often referred to as the "Five W's" and begin with the words:

Who _____?
What _____?
When _____?
Where _____?
Why _____?

Of course, unless you ask questions that have a direct correlation to the needs, pains, and interests of the client, it won't make any difference what type of question you ask. The power of a question lies in whether or not it relates to an area of importance to the buyer, not whether it is yes-no, open, or closed ended.

Cerebral sellers use the following guidelines to determine which question types to use:

- Ask yes-no questions to clarify specific facts
- Ask closed-ended questions for targeted and focused answers
- Ask open-ended questions to gather quantitative information

The Point? Striking an appropriate balance between the three question types is the signature of a professional sales person.

In Summary

In selling situations, talking in terms of the other person's interest is the foundation for effective information gathering. When people see how sellers meet their needs and eliminate their problems, they readily agree to recommended solutions, which is what makes *The DNASelling Method* so effective. It is a logical questioning methodology that guides sellers through the investigation stage of the sales cycle and helps sellers focus their attention on the interests of their prospects. It is a proven, systematic questioning methodology and a refreshing problem-solving approach to selling.

The DNASelling Call Sheet

Account Name:

Discovery Information	Qualification Information
	Decision Maker(s):
	Funding:
	Timeframe(s):
	(Competition):

Needs/Problems	Pains/Consquences

Solutions	Benefits

Figure 12.1

part three

III

POWER PROSPECTING

Dynamic vs. Passive Listening

Learn to listen. Opportunity could be knocking at your door very softly.

—Frank Tyger

———◆———

The saying "Silence is golden," illustrates a fundamental principle observed by all successful businesses. Coca Cola has kept its four-page recipe of the world's best selling soft drink in a guarded bank vault in downtown Atlanta for over one hundred years, and only two executives are allowed access to the recipe. Likewise, the original recipe of Kentucky Fried Chicken is maintained in a time capsule in an undisclosed, guarded area.

Knowing when to be silent has always been an important part of business success. Take, for example, the recent revelations concerning the 1930's film star, Hedy Lamarr, an extremely successful actress in Germany during the rise of the Third Reich. She was renowned for her beauty and talent and was married to a successful Austrian munitions expert who was sympathetic toward the Nazi movement. Unbeknownst to him, his wife was an underground anti-Nazi spy.

Just prior to the outbreak of *World War II*, when Hedy's husband was summoned to Berlin to meet with scientists to find a way to use radio signals to guide torpedoes to their target, the actress insisted on accompanying her husband in his travels. She sat side by side with him as he met with German scientists and Nazi naval officers to identify a way to send a radio signal that could only be received by a designated receiver. They eventually invented a technology called "frequency hopping" that prevented outside listeners from deciphering a message. Mrs. Lamarr absorbed every detail.

Acquiring the frequency information was only the first step in her intelligence efforts and perhaps the easiest. She had to deliver her stolen data to London. Suspicions of her anti-Nazi sentiments had begun to surface, she knew she needed to act quickly. On a scheduled night, she drugged her maid, slipped out of her home, and followed a predetermined route from Austria to London. Once in London, however, she was careful not to reveal too much. After experiencing the nature of espionage and the inherent risks of double agents, she maintained a cautious relationship with her London contacts.

While in London, she happened to meet a Hollywood studio executive she recognized from her acting career and informed him of her espionage activities. She was taken to Washington D.C. to deliver a debriefing to U.S. officials on Nazi intentions. Interestingly, after the debriefing, she filed a secret patent on frequency hopping for wartime communication. Mrs. Lamarr realized that it was technology ahead of its time. Today it is referred to as "spread spectrum technology" and is used in cell phone systems, satellite encryption, and other marvels of modern technology.

Hedy Lamarr's instinct to keep silent and not reveal too much, too soon, to too many people paid off. Neither her patent, nor her espionage activities were publicly revealed until 1990 when a *Forbes* magazine article reported the entire affair.

The Importance of Listening

Hedy Lamarr's experience in espionage can teach us much that is applicable in business and sales today. The first and foremost lesson is that successful salespeople know when to listen and when to talk. The key to Hedy's success, obviously, was knowing when to keep silent.

As fundamental as listening sounds, it seems to be one of the most difficult disciplines to follow, especially for salespeople. This is why the last step of the power benefit statement is to be quiet and listen. Asking effective questions is just one part of the information-gathering process. Listening and understanding the answers is another.

Based on research and observation, I have concluded that the top three problems in sales are:

1. Inadequate questioning and listening skills
2. Engaging in premature presentations
3. Inadequate account qualification

I have also concluded that all three problems can be improved when sellers enhance their listening skills. As fundamental as listening sounds, it seems to be one of the most difficult disciplines to follow, especially for salespeople.

More is not Necessarily Better

The soldiers on the Lewis and Clark expedition (1803-1806) were a sensation to most Indian tribes. William Clark's slave, York, was a special spectacle. His massive size was impressive enough, but the Indians had never seen a black man, and they couldn't make out if he was man, beast, or spirit being.

Because of their inherent novelty, the soldiers enjoyed the favors of the women from most of the Indian tribes, often encouraged to do so by the husbands, who believed that they would catch some of the power of the white men from such intercourse, transmitted to them through their wives. One warrior invited York to his lodge, offered him his wife, and guarded the entrance during the act. York was said to be "the big medicine."

Whether or not the Indian men received power from the intercourse cannot be alleged. It is evident, however, that disease was transmitted. Because of the tribes' hospitality with previous French traders and trappers, venereal diseases were rampant in the villages and passed on to the men of the expedition. It is possible that every man on the expedition suffered from syphilis.

Meriwether Lewis was the only person on the expedition

with any medical experience and treated the disease by having his men ingest mercury in the form of a pill called calomel (mercurous chloride). The mercury pills were sovereign for syphilis, and Lewis knew this and administered it routinely.

Unfortunately, unbeknownst to Lewis, the side effects of ingesting mercury is dangerous; the phrase "mad as a hatter" referred to hat makers who used mercury in the process of their work and became a bit crazy from breathing in the fumes. Compounding the problem was the amount of mercury Lewis was proscribing. He applied all treatments on the principle of *more was better*. How his men survived his treatments is a mystery to modern medical professionals.

———————

Like the primitive medical notion that more is better, many salespeople adhere to the mistaken perception that the more information they provide buyers the better. Average sellers believe they should dominate and control conversations by describing and explaining how wonderful their products or services are, but nothing could be further from the truth. The fastest way to turn off a buyer is to talk, talk, talk. Successful sellers don't dominate conversations with talk; instead, they dominate conversations with good questioning and listening skills.

Contrary to popular belief, the best sales professionals are not the best talkers, but the best listeners. As Stephen R. Covey puts it in *The 7 Habits of Highly Effective People*, highly effective people "Listen with the intent to understand, not to respond." It's no different for successful sellers because great sellers are great communicators, and great communicators are great listeners.

> **Note:** Great sellers dominate listening, not talking.

The Listen-to-Talk Ratio

A frequently asked question I receive during sales training is, "If you don't talk about product or service capabilities, how will the client know what you do?" I'm not suggesting product or service capabilities should not be discussed in the initial sales call. Obviously, product or service capabilities and benefits need to be explained and promoted. What I'm recommending, however, is balance. Since most sellers talk too much and listen too little, their listen-to-talk ratio is out of balance.

If you were to envision a balance scale in front of you with one side representing how much you talk and the other *side how much you listen, which side would the scale favor?*

Listening

Talking

Figure 13.1

Have you ever heard of someone talking himself or herself out of a sale? On the contrary, have you ever heard of someone listening himself or herself out of a sale?

It happens every hour of every day; salespeople talk themselves out of sales. Sellers talk too much, explain too much, interrupt too much, and listen too little.

> **Note:** The Bible tells of Samson killing ten thousand Philistines with the jawbone of an ass. Thousands of sales are killed each day with the same weapon.

I spoke to a potential client who owns a very large, privately held insurance company with branches in multiple cities across California. We were meeting to discuss ways in which we could increase his sales and expand his business, and we had only one hour to make our presentation. We started off the meeting with questions about his business, market, clients, competition, and potential for future growth. We had been meeting with this gentleman for forty-five minutes and had barely mentioned our consultative services. My colleague looked panicked. So I stopped asking questions, put my pen down on my notepad and told the potential client that I would like to take a few minutes and discuss how *Patrick Henry & Associates* could help him achieve his business and sales objectives. Using the information he provided, and utilizing his explanations of potential areas for improvement and growth, I proceeded to explain exactly how we could improve his business and grow his sales exponentially. It took less than ten minutes. We ended our meeting on time, shook hands, and left.

We were awarded the contract.

As we were driving away, I asked my colleague how he thought the meeting went. When he told me he was surprised that I hadn't talked about our training and coaching services until the very end of the conversation (he thought I "cut it too tight) I explained to him that the sale was made prior to the discussion about our training and coaching capabilities when we listened to the owner of the company articulate the problems he was experiencing in growing his company. By the time I discussed *Patrick Henry & Associates*, the owner had convinced *himself* that something needed to be done to address the business and sales challenges he was facing.

My colleague learned a valuable lesson that day about the power of listening. Asking good questions, taking notes, and keeping our mouths shut won the sale.

> **Note:** Average sellers talk. Elite sellers listen.

In our trainings, I often ask people what the appropriate balance should be between listening and speaking. We normally get an array of answers ranging between 70 and 80 percent for listening and 20 to 30 percent for talking. Inevitably, someone brings up the overused saying about God giving us two ears and one mouth. Surprising to many, I fall on the other side of the fence. Even though I'm a huge advocate of listening, and I emphasize its importance, I don't think setting unrealistic expectations is healthy or wise.

When I was first introduced to corporate America, I received some of the finest sales training that existed at the time. The company that recruited me out of college had a very dynamic sales manager who was a skilled professional who taught our sales team the fundamentals of selling, much of which I still utilize to this day. Nonetheless, one of the principles he taught that I later rejected was the 80/20 rule, which states that sellers should spend 80 percent of their time listening and 20 percent of their time talking. I took this rule at face value and tried to implement it. Within a few weeks, I realized it was a quixotic principle—noble cause, but unrealistic in application.

Instead of trying to live up to some listen-to-talk ideal, I learned that balance is the key. By balance I mean that listening needs to balance talking. Sellers should ask themselves, "Do I listen as much as I speak?" "Is my listen to talk ratio balanced?"

Talking  Listening

Figure 13.2

The Point? There is no exact listen-to-talk ratio. Our general rule at *Patrick Henry & Associates* is to *listen at least as much as you talk.* The listen-to-talk ratio should never fall below 50/50.

Dynamic vs. Passive Listening

An attractive woman once attended dinner with distinguished British statesman, William Gladstone. The next evening, she attended dinner with Gladstone's political rival and equally distinguished opponent, Benjamin Disraeli. Asked her opinion of the two men, she replied thoughtfully, "When I left the dining room after sitting with Mr. Gladstone, I thought he was the cleverest man in England, but after sitting with Mr. Disraeli, I thought I was the cleverest woman in England."

One of the benefits of being a good listener is making other people feel important. As noted author Dale Carnegie stated, "The secret of influencing people lies not so much in being a good talker as in being a good listener. Most people, in trying to win others to their way of thinking, do too much talking themselves. Let the other people talk themselves. They know more about their business or problems than you do. So ask them questions. Let them tell you a few things."

There are two general types of listeners: dynamic and passive.

1. Dynamic listeners are focused, alert, and center discussions on the needs and interests of others.

2. Passive listeners are casual, indifferent, and focus discussions on themselves.

Obviously, dynamic listeners are better sellers. Using dynamic listening skills, they enrich and deepen sales conversations with strategic questions that motivate prospective clients to talk. Dynamic listeners also unearth more needs and problems to match to core competencies and proposed solutions. They generate more leads, qualify more accounts, make better presentations, and close more sales. Dynamic listeners are dynamic sellers.

Passive listeners, on the other hand, are not as successful as dynamic listeners because they fail to fully engage buyers and unearth important account issues or critical needs. Neglectful of qualifying accounts, they also fail to match core capabilities with critical needs. Because they are not patient, they interrupt buyers, jump in before knowing the facts, and engage in premature presentations. Not surprisingly, they tend to be arrogant "know-it-alls" who are condescending toward buyers. In short, passive listeners are passive sellers.

> **Caution!** Many sellers are uncomfortable with silence. As a result, they start talking to fill the silence with noise. Resist this temptation. If you don't fill the silence with "talk," the prospect will fill the silence with valuable information.

Listening and Prospecting

The dangers associated with poor listening are too numerous to list and would be difficult to exaggerate. Poor listeners often do more harm than good. They actually turn buyers off by talking too much.

Many people seem to believe that a cold call is somehow separate from the rest of the selling process, but I believe that listening in the initial cold call is at least as important, and in some cases even more important, than in post-prospecting calls because the initial call sets the tone for the rest of the sale. It establishes expectations and forms the foundation of the buyer-seller relationship.

In Summary

Your ears will out earn your mouth.

—Jim Meisenheimer

The charge of the Light Brigade, in which the British cavalry attacked overwhelming Russian gunfire at the battle of Balaclava, was an extraordinary example of military discipline and valor. The improvident heroism, however, resulted in near total annihilation. Watching the doomed advance of his allies, General Pierre Bosquet lamented, *"C'est magnifique, mais ce n'est pas la guerre."* (It's magnificent, but it's not war.)

In like manner, *telling is not selling*. Regardless of how brilliant, eloquent, or articulate a person's words might be, if sellers neglect to listen and truly understand the needs and perspectives of buyers, they are destined to fail.

When engaged in a conversation, give prospects 100 percent of your attention. Take notes, jot down questions, and concentrate on the conversation. When a prospect is speaking, let him or her know that you are listening with statements such as, "I see," or "I understand."

The number one shortcoming and inadequacy of salespeople is not listening dynamically. Instead, they engage in the traditional selling disease of "enough about you—let's talk about me." Be a dynamic listener by practicing "silent selling" skills and hearing the buyer out. Avoid the temptation to cut buyers off and jump in with capability statements. Don't put the beginning of your sentence in the middle of the buyer's sentence. Remember that consultative sellers are brisk and professional, not antagonistic.

> **The Point?** A poor salesperson is a poor listener. A good salesperson is a good listener. A great salesperson is a great listener. Master sellers are master listeners.

CHAPTER 14

Bold Alternatives to Traditional Cold Calls

⟶⟫●⟪⟵

Southwest Airlines is a phenomenal success story. While most airlines struggle to be profitable in any given year, Southwest Airlines has been profitable every year since 1972. Even with the demise of personal and business travel following September 11th, 2001, Southwest Airlines managed to be profitable while many of their competitors declared bankruptcy or looked to Uncle Sam, i.e., U.S. taxpayers, to solve their financial problems.

Why has Southwest Airlines been so successful and to whom is credit given? One man: Herb Kelleher, the chairman, president, and CEO of Southwest Airlines. He was one of the original pioneers who started Southwest Airlines on March 15, 1967.

From the beginning, Southwest Airlines was different from its competitors. They bucked traditional rules of travel, defied conventional wisdom, ignored industry norms, and rejected fashionable management programs. Herb Kelleher knew that to break into the highly competitive airline industry he would have to establish a bold and daring corporate culture that used maverick principles of business and management to outthink, outmaneuver, and outperform competitors. He became intensely involved, even obsessed, by surrounding himself with talented people who were not afraid to deviate from the standard modus operandi of airline travel.

Even his recruiting practices were completely unconventional. He wanted to work around people who were fun, so in 1978 he mandated that his People Department hire people with a sense of humor. "I want flying to be a helluva lot of fun!" In short, fun was taken very seriously at Southwest Airlines. His theory was that humorous environments make the workplace more enjoyable and, therefore, more productive. It worked. Rather than interacting with stiff, boring, or "terminally professional" flight attendants, Southwest Airline passengers are subject to comical PA announcements, playful preflight tricks (such as popping out of an overhead bin), and even an occasional happy birthday song for a lucky passenger.

Southwest Airlines is successful because its employees are smart, bold, and unconventional. They risk intelligently, "color outside of the lines," and make flying original, fresh, and fun.

———————

Be Bold and Original

Like Southwest Airlines, salespeople need to "think outside the box" to be successful prospectors. They need to separate from the pack by being bold and original rather than ending up sounding like carbon copies of each other.

Bold, alternative cold calls seek to gain a buyer's attention by using an approach that is totally unique. Four bold and original approaches include:

1. The Walk Away Approach
2. The Brutally Honest Approach
3. The Ten Second Sound Bite
4. The "Out" Approach

Each alternative approach is used as a preface to the power benefit statement and should not be viewed as its replacement. Bold alternative approaches are used to get your foot in the door, gain the attention of the buyer, and ensure that you are speaking with the right person.

> **Caution!** Bold, alternative opening statements are more risky than traditional opening statements. However, in many cases they are also more effective.

The Walk Away Approach

Many sellers view cold calling as a game of verbal manipulation and twisted strategy to gain a buyer's attention. These are the people who give selling a bad name. The walk away approach is a prospecting method that attempts to eliminate the stereotypic reputation of cold callers. The purpose of this approach is to sound and behave in a way that eliminates the natural instinct of a buyer to get off the phone. The walk away approach is based on the negotiation principle of not sounding needy or desperate. *Patrick Henry & Associates* refers to this principle as the Power of OPS (Options, Prerogatives, or the Status Quo).[1]

Sellers who exercise the power of OPS communicate confidence and strength. People have more confidence in purchases they make from confident people. People like to buy from strong sellers and strong businesses. It's just a natural part of the human psyche. We like to buy from people who project strength. We like to buy from people and businesses in high demand. Sheepish sellers and weak companies do not provide buyers with confidence or a sense of certainty regarding the purchase.

During the Renaissance, there was an abundance of talented artists. There was, however, a shortage of patrons willing to finance the artists. The primary obstacle to an artist's success was finding the right patron. Michelangelo was no exception.

Fortunately, Michelangelo was not only a master painter, he was also a master businessman. His patron was Pope Julius II. The Pope hired Michelangelo to build a marble tomb. The two of them quarreled over the design of the tomb, and Michelangelo left Rome in a fit of disgust. This was a major act of defiance on the part

---

1. See Chapter 4 in *Sales-Side Negotiation* for an in-depth analysis of the six sources of seller-negotiator power.

of Michelangelo. At the time, the Pope represented God's power on Earth.

To the amazement of the papal court, however, the Pope did not fire Michelangelo. Instead, he begged the famed artist to return. He realized that Michelangelo could find another patron, but that he could not find another Michelangelo.

It is important that sellers do not appear weak, desperate, or obsequious to buyers. Buyers who perceive weakness have less respect for the seller, are less responsive to requests, and are more aggressive when making demands.

By utilizing the walk away approach, sellers not only project strength, they also negate a buyer's inclination to be defensive or adversarial. By inviting the buyer to say "No" you actually increase the likelihood of the buyer to say "Yes."

Similar to Isaac Newton's third law of motion that states for every action there is an equal and opposite reaction, the more pressure a seller exerts, the more pressure the buyer exerts back. It's an instinctive response: the harder sellers push, the harder prospects push back.

People have a tendency to respond in a contrarian manner when they feel pressured or manipulated. It's called the *polar affect*. For example, if I say, "I am extremely good looking." Your instinctive response is, "The heck if you are!" Or if I say "I am the best basketball player in town." Your instinct is to respond, "You couldn't beat my little sister in a game of horse!" Buyers respond similarly when sellers make statements such as, "We have the best product on the market, that's why you need to meet with me next Monday." Or "We offer the finest service in the industry. Will Friday morning or afternoon work best for you?" Salespeople generate counterproductive responses by making statements that project pressure.

The Point? By using the walk away approach sellers eliminate pressure.

Examples of the Walk Away Approach

"Hi Ms. Wallace, this is David Zimmerman with ABC Corporation. We provide XYZ services for manufacturers. The purpose of my call is simply to explore any potential fit between our services and your manufacturing needs. Quite frankly, I'm no sure that a fit exists. If not, just tell me and I'll be on my way, but if whoever is in charge of your quality control..."

"Hi Ms. Davenport, this is Jeremy with ABC Corporation. I'm calling because I believe we can decrease your firm's accounting costs—perhaps by as much 20%. Quite frankly, I'm not sure at this point if what we do fits with your company. I just don't know. So if this doesn't make any sense, just tell me and I'll get off the phone. Is that fair?"

"Good morning Mr. Williams, this is John with ABC Corporation. We are the developer of XYZ product. I have no idea whether what we do has any relevance for your business. If not, just tell me and I'll be on my way, but if whoever currently handles your I.T. needs..."

"Good afternoon Mr. Finnegan, this is Chad Lawson with Patrick Henry & Associates. We've recently been working with sales managers in the area of prospecting and have been able to help our clients overcome the challenges their salespeople experience cold calling. Quite frankly, I'm not sure at this point if we can do the same thing for your business, but I'm confident we can. Are you available to meet next Tuesday morning at 9:20?"

By making a walk away statement such as, "I don't know whether or not you have a need or an interest in our product" you let the buyer know that you are not desperate for business and that you are not trying to force something down their throat.

The same rules and habits of good negotiation are applicable to cold calling. By utilizing the walk away approach, sellers exercise the power of OPS and increase their likelihood for success.

The Brutally Honest Approach

The brutally honest approach seeks to "response block" the traditional buyer response of "Oh no, not another underhanded salesperson!" The absolute last thing buyers expect from a cold caller is for them to admit it's a sales call, so use this to your advantage. The shock of being the recipient of such brutal honesty is appealing to many buyers. Remember that the Bible teaches, "The truth shall set you free." Tell the truth from the start and you can gain the confidence and respect of buyers.

> **Note:** One of the ultimate sales weapons is truth. Buyers find blatant truth a refreshing change from many of the shady sales practices and techniques they experience from less than forthright sellers.

Example of a Brutally Honest Approach

"Hi Ms. Jones, this is Danielle with ABC Corporation and this is a sales call."

If buyers respond negatively, they were more than likely going to respond negatively anyway, regardless of what you said. If the buyer responds positively, carry on with the five-step power benefit statement.

Many sales professionals sell in saturated markets in which buyers are bombarded with sales calls every day. In mature markets, buyers have heard literally hundreds of sales calls. Because these buyers have "heard it all before," they end up lumping all sellers into one big class of people. All sellers become one giant blur, and it becomes increasingly difficult for sellers to stand out and avoid being linked to competitors. The brutally honest approach attempts to make a distinct impression and gain a buyer's attention in a bold and professional way.

The Ten Second Sound Bite

In many markets, sellers deal with very blunt, very terse buyers in which even thirty to forty-five second opening statements can be too long. For sellers involved with extremely blunt buyers, or when you are not sure whether or not you are dealing with a decision-maker, the *Ten Second* sound bite is an ideal solution.

The *Ten Second* sound bite is a lightning quick opening statement designed for salespeople who engage with buyers infamous for having little tolerance for sellers (although it can be used in any industry).

The *Ten Second* sound bite is a prospecting model that utilizes three brief sentences designed to "get your foot in the door" and identify decision-makers. To utilize the *Ten Second* sound bite, simply fill in the template below with your information:

> *"Hi* [client name], *this is* [your name] *with* [your business name]. *We are the people who* [state the problems you solve]. *With whom in your organization should I speak?"*

For example, at *Patrick Henry & Associates* we use the following *Ten Second* sound bite:

> *"Hi Ms. Jones, this is Steve Gustin with Patrick Henry & Associates. We are the people who help businesses like yours increase sales with totally unique sales and marketing strategies. With whom in your organization should I speak?"*

The *Ten Second* sound bite is not only quick and easy; it also helps you get to the right person. In order to get the maximum return on your calls, it's critical that you deal with decision makers as early in the sale as possible, so by asking, "With whom in your organization should I speak?" you either confirm the person you are speaking to is the right person, or you will be passed on to whoever is. Qualifying (or disqualifying) a person early in the sale ensures that you don't waste time, investment, money, or energy on people who can't make a decision or purchase your product.

The "Out" Approach

Many sellers feel more comfortable releasing tension early in the sales call by offering potential buyers an "out." The "out" approach is based on the premise that "You can't lose what you don't have." The rationale behind the "out" approach is simple; by extending buyers the courtesy of picking the best time to speak rather than jamming the call down their throats, they will be more open and receptive to your call.

Many buyers have built up strong immune systems against pushy salespeople. We've all been recipients of cold calls in which sellers interrupted our day without an explanation or apology and talk incessantly for what seemed like hours. These kinds of calls drive us crazy and make us reluctant to receive cold calls. The "out" approach is designed to overcome this resistance. By offering buyers the ability to pick a better time to talk, sellers disarm the instinctive propensity of buyers to end unsolicited sales calls.

One reason people dread receiving cold calls is that they feel powerless because they feel as if the seller is in the driver's seat, controlling their time. They don't want to be rude and hang up, but at the same time they are busy and don't really have time to speak at that particular moment. Subsequently, they wait for the seller to pause and then say, "No thank you" and hang up. Because they are busy and have other things to do, they often create their own "out."

The "out" approach addresses this problem head on. By extending buyers an opportunity to say "No," you also extend the opportunity for them to say, "Yes." By empowering buyers to set the time of the call, you put them in the driver's seat because now they can pick the date and time that's best for them. Contrary to what many sellers think, offering buyers an "out" can actually increase the likelihood for advancing the sale.

Examples of an "Out" Approach

"Hi Ms. Thomas, this is Brady McCoy with Patrick Henry & Associates. Is this a bad time to speak?"

"Hi Roger, this Jill with ABC Corporation. Did I catch you at a bad time?"

If the buyer responds negatively, simply say, "When would be a good time to call back?" This is a simple, straightforward, no nonsense way of determining the best time to call back. If the buyer responds positively, carry on with the power benefit statement. If the buyer responds with another time to call back, such as "Call me back tomorrow," say, "Thank you. I will call you tomorrow at 10 A.M." By stating a specific time you are going to call back, it forces the buyer's hand. He or she will either agree with the specified time or will provide you with another time to call back.

Like most alternative approaches, the "out" approach is a preface to the power benefit statement, not a replacement for it.

Many sellers are reluctant to offer prospective buyers an "out" because they fear that by giving buyers an excuse to get off the phone, they are willingly ending their sales opportunity prematurely. They fear that buyers will take the "out" and end their chance to make the sale. While it is true that some prospects will take the "out" and end the call, it is equally true that many buyers will appreciate the fact that you are cognizant of the value of their time and courteous enough to allow them to pick the best time to talk.

As previously addressed, the harder sellers push, the harder prospects push back. When sellers sound pushy, there is an instinctive tendency for buyers to resist and push back. Consequently, by offering a buyer an opportunity to set another time to speak, you circumvent this tendency. You defuse their resistance and create a pressure-free environment by getting their permission to proceed with the call.

The most dreaded response for any cold caller is to be hung up on. There is something about having someone slam the phone down that is disconcerting to our psyches, an affront to our pride. One way to avoid being hung up on is to avoid making pushy sales calls. By using the "Out" approach, sellers provide buyers with an opportunity to say "not right now." This approach helps sellers avoid sounding pushy and disarms a buyer's instinct to hang up.

The "Out" approach also projects confidence. In our negotiation trainings, *Patrick Henry & Associates* teaches sellers the role and importance of power in buyer-seller relationships.[2] By giving a prospective buyer an opportunity to pick a better time to speak, you convey that you are not a desperate seller trying to pry every last penny you can out of anyone willing to listen. By not sounding desperate, you build power and project confidence.

> **The Point?** Use bold alternative cold call strategies to generate interest and distance yourself from traditional telemarketing stereotypes.

---

2. See Chapter 3 in *Sales-Side Negotiation* for information regarding the role of power in sales and negotiation.

CHAPTER 15

Introductory Presentations

———————

In 1980 IBM was searching for an operating system to run its first personal computer. A group of IBM officials scheduled a trip to meet with the president of Digital Research, Gary Kildall. Digital Research led the personal computer software industry with its CP/M operating system. Fatefully, on the day of the scheduled meeting, Kildall decided to go fly his small hobby airplane. Feeling snubbed, IBM decided to head north to meet with a small company in Seattle called Microsoft.

During its initial meeting, IBM announced its personal-computer designs to the president of Microsoft, Bill Gates. Gates was then provided with an opportunity to introduce his technology and boldly suggested that IBM rethink its strategy of using 8-bit processor architecture, recommending instead that they use the new 16-bit processor. Gates knew that if IBM chose to use the new 16-bit processor that they would also need a new operating system to run it. IBM took his advice, decided to use the 16-bit processor and awarded Gates the right to provide an operating system—an operating system Gates did not have!

The amazing part of this historic meeting between IBM and Microsoft is that Bill Gates did not show, demonstrate, or display his technology. He couldn't because he didn't own it yet. Instead, he used the initial meeting as an opportunity to simply introduce his proposed technology and services. The rest is history.

———————

Presentation Types

In contrast to teleselling, teleprospecting calls do not attempt to make one-call sales. Instead, they attempt to either qualify leads or set appointments. Because teleprospecting calls involve more than one meeting to make a sale, normally more than one presentation is required. (See *Figure* 15.1, *The SONAR Selling Map*).

Business-to-business and business-to-consumer presentations are the most common form of sales presentations and are broken down into two categories:

1. Introductory Presentations
2. Solution Presentations

Each presentation addresses a different stage in the sales cycle and has a different objective. For example, years ago when I was selling educational software, I cold called a technical coordinator for a school district in San Francisco, California. I initially used my cold calling script to gain the interest of the buyer and deliver an *introductory* presentation. After briefly describing our software package, I asked a few discovery-qualification and need-problem questions. Obviously both interested and qualified, I proceeded to provide a more detailed description of the capabilities of our software program. When he saw the potential benefits of our product, the technical coordinator invited me to deliver a presentation to his colleagues in the district. I accepted the invitation, but before traveling to San Francisco, I called each of his colleagues. Using need-problem questions (see Chapter 11) I identified the specific needs and problems of the decision makers. Using the information I acquired in my pre-presentation phone calls, I delivered a *solution* presentation that matched our software solutions to the exact problems being experienced throughout the district. By showing how our software program solved their exact problems, I built enormous power, circumvented my competitors, and the committee unanimously selected our product.[1]

---

1. For more information concerning how to deliver exceptional sales presentations, see *Winning Presentations.*

The Introductory Presentation

The initial introduction of goods and services is called an introductory presentation. As part of the initial prospecting call, some type of product or service introduction has to be made in order for buyers to grasp the nature and purpose of the call. The introductory presentation is the portion of the cold call in which sellers introduce the product and explain how it will potentially address the needs of the prospect.

The introductory presentation typically follows either the opening benefit statement or discovery-qualification questions and is exactly what it sounds like—an introduction. It's not an in-depth, elaborate, or detailed presentation. Its purpose is to familiarize prospects with the general characteristics of goods and services and to solicit interest. That's it. It is typically a fairly quick presentation. Most teleprospecting presentations are scripted. The script highlights the core features and characteristics of the proposed good or service so that buyers can quickly grasp the potential capabilities and agree to continue the call.

The purpose of the introductory presentation is to *introduce* capabilities, not *demonstrate* capabilities. Its purpose is to elicit buyer interest in product or service capabilities and to establish credibility, nothing more. Like Bill Gates' presentation to IBM, the initial presentation is meant to familiarize prospects with the potential benefits of a good or service and advance the sale.

Once sellers gain the attention of buyers in the initial meeting, they should ask questions (using *The DNASelling Method*), identify the needs, problems, and primary buying motives of buyers, and focus on acquiring information, not disseminating information.

> **Note:** The introductory presentation is quick, fast, and to the point. It's not meant to be a doctoral thesis. It's meant to be the "pre-game" show that grabs the attention and curiosity of buyers.

The Solution Presentation

Once products and services have been introduced, buyers determine whether or not they see value in continuing the conversation or sale. For sellers engaged in prospecting activities, such as cold calling or attempting to set up appointments, setting up a solution presentation is usually the point or purpose of the call.

The solution presentation is conducted after the investigation stage of the sales cycle and after the needs and problems (the primary buying motives) of buyers have been identified. Without knowing the needs and problems of buyers, sellers cannot make informed recommendations or demonstrate clear and compelling benefits. The solution presentation typically (not always) occurs later in the selling process and is used to match solutions and benefits to specific buyer needs, pains, and problems identified earlier in the sales process. *In other words, the solution presentation moves presentation content from the general to the specific.*

Solution presentations are exact, not generic. They hammer exclusively on what is important and relevant to individual buyers since product features and capabilities are of no value to a buyer unless they address their specific needs or problems. The solution presentation provides buyers with convincing reasons to purchase proposed products and solutions by demonstrating how they will fill needs and solve problems.

Sellers often find themselves with limited presentation opportunities. When necessary, it is possible to combine both presentation types—introductory and solution presentations—into one meeting. However, for prospecting purposes, typically the introductory presentation is sufficient to set an appointment or qualify a lead.

Prospecting Versus Presenting

The purpose of a prospecting call is to qualify a lead or set an appointment, and to advance the buyer to the next stage of the sales cycle. It is not to tell the buyer every possible capability or benefit available with your good or service.

The SONAR Selling Map[2]

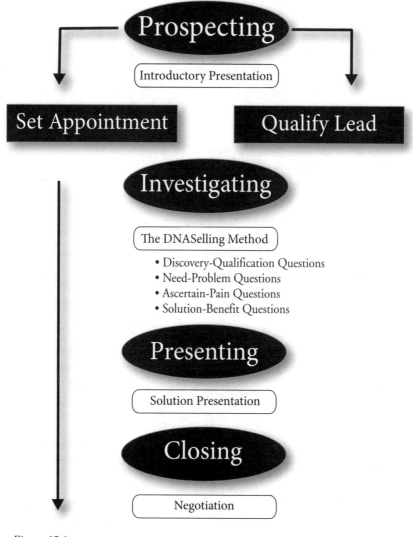

Figure 15.1

2. For more information regarding the four stages of the selling cycle see *The DNASelling Method*, *Winning Presentations*, and *Sales-Side Negotiation*.

There is a tendency for sellers to emphasize products and services too soon in the communication process. Before they have even asked questions about the buyer's situation, many sellers start rattling off solutions that may or may not fit a prospect's needs.

Once the benefit statement is completed, the majority of the conversation should be spent asking questions and listening, not giving a laundry list of features or capabilities. Sellers should introduce products, services, and capabilities and make an introductory presentation, but they should avoid jumping into a premature solution presentation prior to asking need-problem questions.

In Summary

Sellers should focus the majority of the initial sales call on asking questions. Questions demonstrate concern for the prospect's needs and problems and put the focus of the sales call where it belongs—on the prospect.

This is hard medicine to swallow, but the essence of sales maturity is a professional's capacity to delay responses, question, and listen. Cerebral selling requires self-control and the discipline to not "show up and throw up."

CHAPTER 16

Phone, Fax, Voice Mail, and Email

⸺≪●≫⸺

John Colter was a central figure on the Lewis and Clark expedition and went on to become one of the most famous mountain men in U.S. history. He is credited for discovering what is known today as Yellowstone National Park. On a spring day in 1808, while conducting business on behalf of the U.S. government with a Native American tribe, the Crows, the Crows' traditional enemy, the Blackfeet, attacked. Although Colter escaped, the Blackfeet held a grudge against him from that moment on.

Months later, while canoeing on the Jefferson River with a companion named Potts, Colter became nervous as they ventured deep into Blackfeet territory. He had good reason for his edginess because suddenly several hundred Blackfeet Indians surrounded them on each side of the river. The chief of the Indians ordered the trappers to come ashore. Colter, realizing the chief could have them killed at any moment, acquiesced and went ashore. The second he touched shore, dozens of squaws ripped his clothes off. Completely naked and weaponless, he instantly found himself standing in front of hundreds of screaming warriors.

The chief demanded that Potts come ashore as well. Potts refused. An Indian warrior then shot Potts in the arm. Potts returned fire and killed the Indian who shot him. While attempting to reload his rifle, the Blackfeet warriors swarmed Potts and savagely beat him to death.

The screaming Indians then turned their fury on Colter who, although he took numerous blows to the head, remained conscious. The chiefs of the tribe argued over what to do with their captive until they decided that he would be hunted like an animal. One of the chiefs walked up to Colter, took him by the arm, led him to a field, and signaled to Colter to start running. Knowing it was his only possible means of escape, he dashed off across the flatlands. Within minutes he heard the haunting noise of approaching Indian warriors. Perhaps no runner ever had more of an incentive to run than John Colter. Fortunately, Colter was an excellent runner and kept up a grueling pace. One by one all but one of the exhausted Indians fell behind. Colter knew he would not be able to outrun this particular Indian, so he stopped and faced the oncoming warrior. Without hesitation, the warrior charged, raised his spear, and lunged toward Colter. Colter side stepped the Indian, grabbed the spear, and threw him to the ground.

After killing his attacker, Colter took what belongings he could carry and began running again. Aware that he would not be able to outrun or outfight all of the pursuing Indians, he used nature to escape. He came to a river and swam out to a small island where he hid under a pile of tangled driftwood. Within minutes dozens of Indians were running up and down the riverbank.

They eventually swam out to the island and began probing each hiding place with their spears, continuing even after nightfall. Freezing and under the cover of darkness, Colter slipped out of his hiding spot and carefully swam downstream. He eventually emerged from the river, but instead of crossing the mountain pass—which would have been guarded by Indians—he climbed the nearly vertical slopes of a distant ridge and spent the next eleven days concealing himself by day and traveling by night, eating nothing but roots and plants. He eventually stumbled into a trapper's fort where his fellow trappers scarcely recognized him.

Colter's miraculous escape was due in large part to his resourcefulness. Whatever resources and opportunities that were available, he used to survive including terrain, rivers, driftwood, darkness, and even an Indian's spear.

Obstacles or Opportunities?

In sales, optimum environments and perfect scenarios do not always present themselves. In many cases the opposite is true—obstacles are put in our path. But more often than not, perceived obstacles are hidden opportunities. Like John Colter's miraculous escape, how we choose to use those opportunities is up to us.

In today's complex world of communication, successful sellers utilize numerous methods of contact to generate qualified leads and set appointments. They take advantage of every opportunity by using whatever medium of communication is available including phone, fax, voice mail, and email.

Effective Voice Mail Messages

Between voice mail, automated attendants, and caller identification systems, doing business on the phone is more challenging than ever. It's increasingly difficult to reach people because it's becoming easier for them to avoid us.

For many sellers, the number one medium for contacting prospective clients is voice mail. Many sellers experience two or three times as many voice mails as they do voice-to-voice conversations. Unfortunately, many sellers downplay leaving voice messages and consider them a waste of time. They view voice mail as an enemy—the evil gatekeeper. Salespeople are often taught that leaving voice mails is useless, and they are instructed to *not* leave them. In most cases (especially with business-to-business calls), this is a mistake. Although it is true that a majority of voice messages will not be returned (this is not a phenomena reserved to sales calls), when prospects do call back they are almost always qualified and convert into sales.

Surprisingly, when we survey our trainees, a large percentage of them claim to hang up on voice mails rather than leave messages. This is a decision I have a hard time understanding because what is the chance a prospect will call us back if we don't leave a message? Zero. On the other hand, if we leave a message, we automatically increase the odds that we will receive a return phone call.

In most cases, voice mail can actually be a bridge instead of a barrier. Many successful sellers prefer to leave voice messages because they have higher success ratios in less time. Leaving a voice message is fast, and it also preliminarily qualifies a buyer. Because many buyers use voice mail as a way to screen calls, when they call back, they are obviously interested in your product or service; you have "struck a nerve."

Voice mails (like emails) are also checked at the leisure of the buyer, thus avoiding the "interruption" factor of cold calling.

I recently consulted a company with a very dynamic CEO. This gentleman was not the average "glass ceiling" CEO. He regularly got into the trenches of his corporation and would drop by the shipping department and help fill orders. If his garbage was full, he emptied it. He even made cold calls! He was extraordinary, so when I began setting up *The SONAR Selling System* for his company, he was on hand for every decision. As the issue of cold calling came up, he made it clear that he did not want his salespeople leaving voice messages. Of course, I questioned his decision and asked him why. He replied that leaving voice messages was a waste of time. When I pressed him a bit further, he stated he had never had a prospect call him back after leaving a voice mail. After listening to his response, I told him I thought we should still leave voice messages. He gazed at me with an incredulous look on his face that conveyed something to the effect of, "Did you not just hear what I said? How could a person like you call himself cerebral!" So I made him a gentleman's wager. I told him that I would make one hundred cold calls and leave messages for every lead that put me in voice mail, but I had one stipulation: the return phone number I left had to be his personal cell phone number. He agreed, and sure enough, he received two callbacks the first day. A little over ten days later we were sitting in his office discussing marketing strategies when his cell phone rang. It was a call back from a cold call I made on the first day of our wager.

> **Note:** An alternative way of looking at voice messages is to view them as advertising vehicles. Voice mails give you an opportunity to deliver a message without interruption or objection.

One of the reasons many voice mails are not returned is because most sellers leave the same run-of-the-mill, worn out message that every seller leaves. Traditional voice messages are not effective with busy buyers who hear dozens of the same carbon copy, cold call messages on a regular basis. Unfortunately, most voice messages are facsimiles of each other that simply inject different sellers and company names.

Leaving effective voice messages requires creativity. To be successful, sellers need to implement unconventional tactics to entice buyers to return calls. Because most prospecting calls use the same steps, the same scripts, and the same verbiage, sellers who leave non-traditional voice messages sound unique, and generate curiosity.

Review all of the voice messages sellers recently left in your voice mail. What did they sound like?

Exercise: "Hello, you have reached the voice mail of Will Purdue. I'm not able to take your call at this time, but if you will leave your name and number I'll return your call." (Beep)

What would you say? Write it down.

_____

_____

_____

_____

_____

If you left the above voice message on your own voice mail would you return the call?

If the answer is yes, stick with it. If the answer is no, or if you are not sure, consider creating a more interesting, bolder, and more creative voice mail. The key is to differentiate yourself from the other hundred voice messages your prospective client will get this month.

Pose a Potential Question

One way to differentiate your message from other sales messages is to ask questions. When prospects hear provocative questions, they instinctively want to answer them. During corporate trainings, I emphasize this point with a little exercise. Calling on a participant to come to the front of the room, I ask him or her, "Can I ask you a question?" Without exception they respond with "Sure." They stand there in anticipation of what the question is going to be and so do the rest of the participants.

One way to professionally "provoke" buyers into returning voice messages is to pose provocative questions.

> *"Hello Ms. Smith. My name is Patrick Hansen. My phone number is (888) 888-8888. I have a question I believe only you will be able to answer. I'll be in my office until 5:00 P.M. Please call me back at (888) 888-8888."*

> *"Hi Mr. Jones. My phone number is (888) 888-8888. I'm calling in regard to a question I believe only you can answer. I'll be in my office until 5:00 P.M. If you would, please call me back at (888) 888-8888."*

> **Note:** Always leave your phone number as the first and last thing you say. Say your name and number slowly and clearly.

Do not confuse provocative questions with intellectually insulting or stupid questions. Ridiculous questions such as, "If I could save you a million dollars, would you be interested in meeting with me?" or "Mr. Smith, do you object to making a profit?" should be avoided. Buyers recognize them for what they are—traps.

The Power of Brevity

The most valuable of all talents is that of never using two words when one will do.

—Thomas Jefferson

Most cold callers leave voice messages that sound like the Old Testament. Since traditional voice messages overburden buyers with too much information, simplicity and brevity are essential to leaving effective voicemails.

It seems as though voice messages are returned in inverse proportion to the amount of information left on the voice mail, so avoid overwhelming prospects with too much information. Brief messages and partial information statements allow curiosity to get the best of the buyer.

"Hi Mr. Underhill, this is Jennifer Coats with Patrick Henry & Associates. My phone number is (888) 888-8888. We helped our most recent client, ABC Corporation increase sales over 33 percent. I'm confident we can do the same for you. Please call me at (888) 888-8888. I look forward to hearing from you."

"Hi Mr. Nugent, this is Sharon Moore with Patrick Henry & Associates. My phone number is (888) 888-8888. We help businesses increase sales. Please contact me at (888) 888-8888. I look forward to hearing from you."

"Hi Ms. Liddy, this is Samuel Starks with Patrick Henry & Associates. My phone number is (888) 888-8888. We help businesses increase sales. In fact, we recently increased sales at ABC Company over 20%. I'm confident we can provide similar results for your business. That number again is (888) 888-8888. I look forward to hearing from you."

The Point? Listeners' attention spans are short on the phone. Leave voice messages that are bold, brief, and to the point.

Tell Them Who You're Not

One way to sound unique is to use a little humor in the voice message by telling them who you're not. You might say something like,

"Hi, my name is Patrick Hansen. My phone number is (888) 888-8888. I don't work for the IRS, the Mafia or the CIA. I'm not trying to sell you Tupperware. I'm not looking for a job, and I don't need to borrow money. But I would like to talk to you about how we recently increased sales for ABC Company over 33 percent, and why I'm confident we can do the same thing for you. Please call us, Patrick Henry & Associates at (888) 888-8888."

The Assumptive Voice Mail

Some salespeople leave voice mails (for appointment-based cold calls) that simply assume the buyer will meet with them. For example, many salespeople leave messages such as,

"Hi, this is (your name) with (your business) . My phone number is (888) 888-8888. The purpose of my call today is simply to set up an appointment regarding (X product or issue) . I'll be dropping by for a few minutes next Tuesday morning at 9:20. If this is not a convenient time for us to meet, please call and let me know. My number is 1 (888) 888-8888."

The assumption is that the prospect will meet with you, but will the person you have called show up for the appointment? It's hard to say. Will the person call you back if he or she doesn't want to meet? Maybe. Will the person call back to set up another time that's more convenient? Sometimes. Remember, if you give a time to meet, you have to fulfill your end of the agreement. Don't set a time to meet and then not show up for the appointment.

This is a fairly bold voice mail, and it doesn't work for everyone. Try it out. If it works, stick with it.

How Often Should You Call Back?

My general recommendation is one week. Sellers who call back too soon sound desperate. They inadvertently project an obsequious image, rather than a professional image. When sellers appear desperate for business, they can't negotiate or maneuver from a position of strength. When buyers know sellers are desperate for business, they are less responsive and are more prone to ask for discounts and price concessions.[1] To avoid this problem, don't beg for business or appear overly anxious for their patronage by calling them back too soon.

My general rule is to call back once a week for three weeks with a fourth call on the fifth week. After that, I move on, and I recommend you do the same. There are, however, exceptions to this rule.

I had lunch with a very dynamic business consultant from Florida who told me a story that proved the exception. When he tried to land an account with a major firm in Miami, he left message after message. After numerous voice messages, he decided to turn up the heat because he really wanted this account and refused to give up. Consequently, he called the person again and left the following voice message (with different names of course), "Hi Mr. Dorfman. This is Harry Truman again. I just wanted to let you know that I'm a perfect fit for your company and know that my services will benefit your business. If you give me a half an hour of your time I promise to make it worthwhile. I'm not going to give up until we have a chance to meet. I'm going to call you three times a day, seven days a week until you call me back. My number is 888-8888. I'm not trying to be a pest. I'm trying to earn your business." He kept his promise by calling three times a day and leaving a message with each call. After three or four days, he got his call back, set the appointment, and a short time later made the sale.

Depending on the potential pay off for the time investment, it might make sense to make more than the recommended four return calls.

Prepare Your Voice Mail in Advance

Patrick Henry & Associates regularly works with companies to create

---

1. See *Sales-Side Negotiation* for details concerning how to deal with price demands and buyer negotiation tactics.

cold call scripts and prospecting strategies. One of the most predictable nuisances we face is sellers who think that they sound better when they don't use a script. They are, without exception, wrong. For some reason, this problem is exacerbated when it comes to leaving voice mails. Because many sellers feel that voice mail is somehow completely different from a normal sales call, they "freestyle" their message. Predictably, their voice messages are wordier, longer, and less effective.

I worked with a start up company that received a large amount of investment capital. One of the investors reviewed literature regarding our sales training and consultation services and asked if we would be interested in helping "jump start" the venture. After reviewing the financial numbers and growth potential, we readily agreed. Part of setting up *The Cerebral Selling System* involved establishing an effective prospecting campaign, so we created numerous cold call scripts, tested them on the market for effectiveness, and confirmed a finalized cold call script. We then trained the newly hired salespeople in power prospecting principles, role played the scripts in depth, and sent them selling. As part of our coaching program, we reviewed the calls of each salesperson, and as usual, there were one or two sellers who started going "off road," ignoring the script, and speaking off the top of their heads. Predictably, their calls were longer, wordier, and less effective. They struggled to find the right words, had uncomfortable pauses, uttered too many "uhs," "ahs," and "ums," and lost the opportunity to make a powerful impression. *This became especially apparent with voice mails. When they ignored our customized, strategic voice mail script, their voice mails became cluttered, sometimes even confusing.*

Be sure to prepare your voice mails in advance.

Effective Fax Messages

Cerebral sellers sometimes use unconventional methods to generate leads and set appointments, including the use of fax machines. How many salespeople do you know who incorporate a fax in their prospecting and selling efforts? Most salespeople view the fax as an archaic communication tool. Because most salespeople do not use the fax as part of their selling modus operandi, you should. By using the fax as a means of communication you stand out from competitors and separate yourself from competing vendors.

Fax machines are wonderful tools for communication and can be used for both pre-call correspondence and as a follow-up tool. Similar to an introductory letter, messages can be faxed prior to a cold call to help "warm up" the initial call. You should simply write a brief, personal cover letter that tells the decision maker you'll be calling soon to introduce your good or service.

As a follow up to your call or voice mail, use your fax machine as an additional or alternative way to get through to prospects. After leaving a voice message (or speaking with a gatekeeper), follow up with a fax message. Fax a referral letter from a satisfied customer with a cover sheet that says, "FYI." This is especially effective when the referral letter is from a reputable company in the same industry, perhaps even a prospect's competitor.

> **Note:** To increase the impact of your voice mail, follow it up with a fax message. You might even recommend in your voice message that the buyer check his or her fax machine.

When using fax messages to communicate with buyers, follow some simple guidelines:

1. Keep the fax brief. No one likes receiving long faxes, so don't send an eight-page fax to a prospective client. Keep the fax to one page. I had a caller to my radio program relate a story that makes the point. He told me that he faxed a fairly long, multi-page fax message to a prospective client. But the prospect was apparently so irritated by the length of the fax that he returned the favor, with one small catch. His twenty-five page return fax was entirely blank, and black.

2. Use type sizes that are at least ten points. This ensures your fax message is at a legible minimum.

3. Keep your fax design as clean and simple as possible. Faxes with too much "black space" or too many images and pictures don't fax well. Likewise, faxes that cram every last inch with text are neither inviting nor appealing. Remember that less can be more, so simplify your message with clear language and an obvious call to action.

4. Make certain you include all of the return contact information possible. Your company name, address, telephone number, fax number, web site, and email address should all be clearly visible on the fax.

5. Be creative. Humorous fax messages are attractive, fun, and stand out among sheets of fax messages. Fax a joke to a decision maker and be funny. Clean humor will almost always generate a positive response. By sending a humorous fax message, your fax will stand out among the other sheets of paper on your prospect's desk. WinFax Pro, for example, includes a collection of humorous cover sheets with their fax software that you can customize with your own captions.

Humorous fax transmissions are also an effective way to sway gatekeepers since they are often responsible for picking up faxes and delivering them to the appropriate individuals or departments. Gatekeepers often determine which faxes get placed on the decision-maker's desk and which faxes end up in the garbage bin. Humorous faxes are a great way to make a favorable impression and almost always have a way of making it to the desks of decision makers.

Using faxes as a means of communication offers several advantages. First, with the advent of email, and attaching documents to emails, the number of faxes being received has dramatically decreased. Second, faxes are not in envelopes that are more likely to find a garbage bin than a decision maker's desk. Third, faxes can be sent in the morning and followed up with a phone call the very same day.

By law, fax transmissions must include information that identifies the caller's name, phone number, the date, and time of transmission.

See The Telephone Consumer Fraud Protection Act to ensure compliance with fax transmission laws.[2]

> **Caution!** Know the law. Blindly sending unsolicited, blanket fax messages is against the law without including required information on the fax transmission.

Effective Email Messages

Used appropriately, email is a simple and easy way to communicate with potential clients. Like fax messages, email messages can be used for both pre-call correspondence and as follow-up tools.

Many of the fundamental rules that apply to phone, fax, and voice mail communication also apply to email communication. When using email to communicate with buyers, follow some simple guidelines:

1. Be brief. No one likes long emails (except your mom), and no one reads them.

2. Use proper grammar. Capitalize the first word of each sentence, use appropriate sentence and paragraph lengths, use commas appropriately, and be sure to spell check your message before sending it. Don't expect a first class response from an email that looks like it was sent from a middle school drop out. Communicate that you care and that you are competent.

3. Go easy on exclamation marks !!!!! and email headers set in ALL CAPS. Use email titles and headers that don't sound or look like every other desperate business trying to cajole people into reading their email message. Start your email with a professional, friendly, and courteous header. For example, "Thank you for reading this email," or anything that does not lead people to feel like they have been "e-violated" when they open your email.

---

2. Contact the American Telephone Association for updated information regarding fax transmission legalities.

4. When possible, be personal. Use the person's name and your name. Communicate to the prospect that your message is not a generic email sent to thousands of people.

5. Leave as much return contact information as possible. Be sure to include your return telephone and fax phone number in the email.

The Point? A variety of approaches provides more opportunity to connect with potential buyers. Utilize phone, fax, voice mail, and email to solicit buyer interest, generate leads, and set appointments.

CHAPTER 17

Eliminate Resistance

In the middle of difficulty lies opportunity.

—Albert Einstein

———◆———

In 1836, Mexican dictator Santa Anna led an army of 5,000 soldiers against a tiny band of 180 Texans walled up in an old mission church in San Antonio, Texas, called the Alamo. For close to two weeks, Santa Anna's artillery battered the mission walls with little result. Meanwhile, Sam Houston was recruiting volunteers from all over Texas to repel Santa Anna's punitive expedition.

After two weeks of heavy bombardment, Santa Anna sent one last demand to the heavily outnumbered Texans to surrender. Colonel William Travis answered the demand with a cannonball. Angered at the stubborn resistance of the defiant Texans, Santa Anna ordered his trumpeters to sound the "Diablo," the Mexican signal that no quarter was to be given. They had no choice but to fight to the death. The Texans, including Davy Crocket, initially repelled the Mexican attack, but after three days of hard fighting, the brave Texans were overrun by the Mexican army.

Although the loss of brave men at the Alamo was a devastating blow to the Texas war for independence, it eventually led to the final defeat of Santa Anna. Following his victory at the Alamo, Santa Anna marched his drained and bloodied troops to San Jacinto where Sam Houston's volunteers easily defeated his exhausted men.

———◆———

Overcoming Buyer Resistance

Sometimes to win a war you have to lose a battle. Like the Texan war for independence, the defeat at the Alamo led to the final victory over

Santa Anna at San Jacinto. Likewise, in sales, sometimes an initial set-back can be an opportunity to advance an account and win a sale.

The most difficult challenge sellers face when cold calling is dealing with buyer resistance. One of the primary reasons salespeople fear objections is because they haven't effectively planned for how they are going to handle them. *Preparing in advance to deal with buyer resistance is the most effective way to overcome negative responses.*

There are obviously numerous responses to cold calls, but the five most common negative responses are:

1. "We're really not interested."
2. "Send me some literature."
3. "I'm happy with what I have."
4. "I'm busy right now."
5. "I don't have much time. What's the price?"

Very rarely do prospective clients simply say "No." They usually say something like, "I'm busy right now," "Send me some literature," or "We're really not interested." For that reason, learning to anticipate and overcome common responses is an important part of successful cold calling.[1]

Effective Rejoinders to Cold Call Objections

It's not whether you get knocked down, it's whether you get up.

—Vince Lombardi

Unfortunately, the traditional seller response to buyer resistance is to concede. Most sellers simply give up the moment they hear a negative response. While prospects are on the phone, why not give them one more shot? At that point in the sale, why not take a chance and try to professionally persuade the buyer to listen. What do you have to

---

1. For an in-depth review of how to prevent and overcome sales objections see Chapter 17 in *The DNASelling Method.*

lose? Actually, by not responding appropriately, you lose a great deal. Learning to overcome and eliminate buyer resistance is a skill that could be the difference between becoming a high-earning sales professional and a low-earning sales representative over the lifetime of a sales career.

Developing simple, well-thought-out responses *prior* to cold calling will greatly enhance your ability to eliminate resistance and overcome cold call objections.

> **Note:** Use your script sheet to write down effective rejoinders to common cold call responses. Having effective responses available for reference in the heat of battle increases the likelihood for eliminating resistance.

"We're Really Not Interested."

When buyers say that they are "really not interested," they don't see value in continuing the conversation. The key, therefore, is to inject value into the conversation, quickly and powerfully. How? By dropping the names of other recognizable and reputable companies that will establish credibility and project implied value. Reference an existing client and then mention, in the briefest way possible, how you benefited your referenced company with a product, service, or a result such as a percentage of increased sales or decreased costs.

Buyer: We're really not interested.

Seller: Ms. Prospect, one of my largest clients, ABC Corporation, said the same thing before they had a chance to see how we could benefit them with X product. I promise not to waste your time. Are you available to meet next Tuesday morning at 9:20?

"Send Me Some Literature"

This is probably the most difficult objection to handle because "Send me some literature" is usually a polite way of saying, "Get lost." Most sellers respond to this objection by sending information, believing they have advanced the sale one step further in the sales cycle; however, this is rarely the case. In most instances, the seller is no further along in the sales cycle than he or she was prior to the call, not to mention the added cost of sending the packet.

Buyer: Send me some literature.

Seller: No problem. But before I do I need to ask you a question. To help me tailor literature to your specific needs, tell me about how you currently handle X?

If you send literature, confirm a follow-up date. "I'm going to send you literature that should arrive by Monday. How much time will you need to review it?" After you send the literature, call to confirm receipt and ask "What did you like best about what you reviewed?" The typical response is, "Uh, I haven't looked at it yet." Follow up with, "When do you recommend I call back?"

If you do send literature, don't just hope the buyer will kind of, sort of, hopefully, maybe call you back. Use the literature as a way to springboard an appointment.

Other potential seller responses to "Send me some literature" include:

Seller: Great. I would be glad to drop off some information. I'm going to be in your area on June 10th. What would be a good time to stop by?

Seller: Tim, do you have access to the Internet? [Yes]. Excellent. What I recommend we do is spend a few minutes reviewing information on our Web site together. Our Web address is...

Seller: Mr. Smith, my experience as an ABC consultant has been that sending literature is typically ineffective, so what I would rather do is set up an appointment. Will this Tuesday at 9:20 work for you?

Seller: Tammy, it's no problem, I can send you some literature. But before I do, I need to ask you a question. Sometimes when people ask me to send literature before knowing anything about my service what they are really saying is they just don't have any interest. But they're too nice to tell me because they don't want to hurt my feelings. Is that the case here Tammy?

I know of a salesperson who includes a self-addressed, stamped envelope along with the sales literature. When he conducts his follow up calls, if the buyer says that he has not yet reviewed the material, he responds, "If you're really not interested, that's fine, but that literature is expensive. If you don't mind, would you please mail it back to me?" Apparently, over ninety percent of prospects faced with this choice exhibit a polarity response—that is they do the exact opposite of what is being suggested. By asking them to return the literature, they feel obligated to act on it.

> **Note:** Don't be afraid to disqualify the candidate. You read that right, *disqualify*. The worst possible scenario is for a prospective client to act interested, absorb your time, effort, and money and not purchase your good or service.

"No Thanks. We're Happy with What We Have."

A simple fact in selling is that most people are genuinely satisfied with what they are currently using. If they weren't, they would be calling you. When buyers say, "I'm happy with what I have," what they are saying is that they are satisfied with the status quo.

When I cold called a school district in southern California, the district technical coordinator answered the phone, and I gave her my opening statement. However, when she said to me, "No thank you, we're happy with our current program," I instinctively reacted by saying, "Ms. Smith, that is what everyone tells me until they hear why our product is so much better for their students. I promise not to waste your time. Will you give me just a few minutes to tell you how?" She consented and within a few months I made one of the largest sales our company had ever been awarded. It happened because I did not give up. I used a limited version of the following response to get the appointment.

Buyer: No thanks, we're happy with what we have.
Seller: Mr. Prospect, one of my largest clients, ABC Company,
           responded the same way before they had a chance
           to see how we could benefit them with X product.
           We decreased their production costs by 8%. I don't
           want to waste your time or mine, but I'm confident
           we can realize similar results for your business.

People are often satisfied with what they have because they don't know that something better is available. Many buyers are completely ignorant of other possibilities, capabilities, and options. Use the above rejoinder to let the buyer know that your good or service is valuable. Communicate in a brief sentence how your good or service benefited the referenced company. Then offer an exact date and time to meet.

> **The Point?** All seasoned salespeople have sold to clients who initially stated that they weren't interested. Don't give up after the first negative response.

"I'm Busy Right Now."

This is a tough one since it can be difficult to determine if the buyer is attempting to get rid of you or is legitimately busy at the moment of your call. To combat this dilemma, attempt to use the statement as a way of setting up a future phone or face-to-face appointment.

Buyer: I'm busy right now.

Seller: When would be a good time to call back?

Seller: Ms. Prospect, the only reason I'm calling is to set an appointment. Would next Tuesday morning at 9:20 be a good time for us to meet?

Obviously, in most cases the prospect won't agree to the appointment. Instead, he or she will probably revert back to another traditional response such as, "Why don't you just send me some literature?" Of course, you now know what to say to that response. If the buyer does agree to a call back time, be sure to establish a firm call back date and time. Avoid agreeing to vague commitments such as, "Sure, call me sometime next week."

"I Don't Have Much Time. What's The Price?"

If at all possible, avoid answering price related questions until you have identified client needs and problems. Without first identifying client pains and problems that require resolution, your product or service has little value to the buyer, and without understanding the value of your good or service, you will almost always seem too expensive. To avoid this situation, try to ask at least one qualifying question and then quickly build the value of your product or service before offering a price.

Buyer: I don't have much time. What's the price?

Seller: I'd be glad to quote our prices, but unless you understand what I'm offering it won't make much sense. Would you mind answering a few short questions first?

Seller: I'll be glad to answer that. But first, what do you know about what I'm offering?

Seller: That depends. What is it you need?

If the buyer refuses to answer questions or insists on a price, quote your least expensive price. For instance, you might say, "Our entry-level product, which includes X, costs Y dollars."

The "That's Why" Strategy

Regardless of what objection a buyer poses, many sales professionals find it useful to respond with a simple response called the "That's Why" strategy. No matter what objection a buyer presents, the seller uses the objection to springboard to the next step in the selling process. For example, if a buyer says, "We already have a service," using this strategy a seller responds with, "Well, *that's why* I'm calling." If a prospect says, "I'm happy with my current program" a seller says, "*That's why* I'm calling." If a prospect says, "I don't think that is something we can afford right now," the seller answers with, "Well, *that's why* I'm calling." No matter what objection a buyer presents, the seller simply says, "Well, that's why I'm calling," or "That's why I think we ought to get together." The seller then proceeds with the purpose of the call—to set an appointment or qualify the lead.

The "That's Why" response has perplexed many prospects who thought that they had just shot the seller out of the saddle. When you are not sure how to respond to a prospect's objection, or when in doubt, use the "That's Why" strategy.

Executive Networking

In Chapter 1, I introduced the concept of executive networking to open sales calls. Satisfied customers are a great way to start a buyer-seller relationship.

Executive networking can also be used to overcome objections. Rather than becoming defensive to a prospect who poses objections, let a satisfied customer do your selling for you by serving as a reference or providing a testimonial. If a prospect makes an objection you might say, "I'd like to have one of our customers, Ms. Johnson, call you. She'll tell you how we helped significantly _____."

Utilizing satisfied customers is one of the smartest ways to overcome buyer objections.

In Summary

Preparation is the key to overcoming objections. Ideally, you should never hear an objection to which you don't already have an answer. By memorizing and implementing the previous responses, cold callers increase the probability of successfully eliminating buyer resistance and advancing the call to the next stage of the sales cycle.

There are, of course, some negative responses that sellers will not be able to overcome, but don't despair. Utilize the rejoinders in this chapter to eliminate resistance. If you are still unsuccessful, move on. Don't waste your time arguing with a prospect. Simply say, "Thank you very much, have a nice day," hang up and go on to your next call.

CHAPTER 18

Turn Interest into Action

In 1518, commanding a fleet of eleven ships in search of gold and riches, Hernando Cortez left the island of Cuba to explore the coasts of the Yucatan Peninsula. During his exploration, he stumbled upon a sailor who had been shipwrecked on the peninsula coast some years earlier. The Spaniard told Cortez stories of a vast empire whose dominions extended into the interior of Mexico. The sailor also told Cortez that the empire was renowned for its vast amounts of gold as well as its brutality. Tales of torture and human sacrifice were rampant. A Mexican slave, who had been presented to Cortez as a gift from the natives, confirmed the shipwrecked sailor's claims.

Cortez immediately changed course and headed straight for the coasts closest to the empire, eventually landing on the Mexican coast near modern day Veracruz where he unloaded his horses and supplies. He then made one of the boldest decisions in exploration history—he burned his ships behind him. There would

be no turning back. In an effort to stiffen the will of his men, and to send a clear message of "do or die," he eliminated any means of retreat or escape. Curiosity in gold and glory was suddenly converted into a firm commitment of loyalty and survival.

Using the shipwrecked sailor as a guide and the slave as an interpreter, Cortez led a small army of 15 horsemen and 400 soldiers up the steep slopes leading from the coast to the upland regions of Mexico. He marched straight for the heart of the Aztec Empire and prepared to do battle with the Aztec army. In one of history's most extraordinary battles, Cortez overcame the crushing numerical superiority of his opponents and defeated an army of 40,000 native warriors with only 400 men. Aztec military leaders were astonished at the boldness of Cortez, the power of Spanish firearms, and the might of Spanish horses.

Although historians have questioned the recorded size of the Aztec army, none have questioned the courage of Cortez and his men. Still, Cortez's boldest move was not attacking the numerically superior Aztecs but eliminating any chance for escape by burning his ships behind him. In dramatic fashion, he cemented the courage and commitment of his men with a clear and unmistakable message of "conquer or be conquered."

Obviously dissimilar in fashion, but similar in purpose to the actions of Cortez, sales professionals should do everything in their power to gain a firm commitment from buyers. Those commitments can be large or small, but some sort of commitment or agreed upon action should always be obtained.

Advancing the Sales Call

Effectively closing sales calls is one of the most ignored aspects of cold calling.[1] This is why the objective of every cold call should be to gain some sort of commitment to advance the sale—to get the prospect to take action including responding to an email, reviewing literature, setting up an appointment, or returning a call.

As previously addressed, the purpose of every step of the sales cycle is to advance the prospect to the next stage of the cycle. After a potential buyer takes time to listen, evaluate, and respond to your call, use a commitment-based close to advance the caller to the investigation or presentation stage of the sales cycle.

The Three-Step Close

There are three steps to a commitment-based close:

1. Quickly summarize the call
2. Propose Action
3. Establish the next point of contact

---

1. For a detailed discussion of professional closing methods, see Chapter 20 in *The DNASelling Method.*

By *quickly reviewing the major topics* covered during the call, sellers ensure that buyers clearly understand the topics of discussion. With a quick summary, communication is increased and objectives, purposes, capabilities, and commitments are solidified.

> **Caution!** Keep the call summary brief and to the point.

Proposing action between the buyer and seller is the most important part of the commitment-based close because in order to turn interest into action, some type of action must be initiated and agreed upon. For example, at the conclusion of the call you might establish an appointment date, or for qualification purposes, you might request that the buyer review your Website, respond to a forthcoming email, or agree to a follow-up phone call.

If you are unsure of the next best step, ask the buyer. You might say,

"Ms. Jones, earlier in the conversation we discussed some of the problems you are experiencing with X and how Y can potentially alleviate some of those issues. *Help me understand the next best step to move this project forward.*"

By involving the buyer in the commitment decision, you increase the probability of commitment fulfillment. Asking the buyer what "the next best step is," is an extremely effective question. An equally effective question is "What do you want to happen next?"

After you gain agreement to a proposed action, *establish the next point of contact.* Avoid vague commitments to future communication such as, "I'll call you sometime next week." Instead, establish firm and specific dates, times, and locations for follow up. Don't end a call without first determining how and when you will next communicate. Always establish the next point of contact.

Sellers who conclude their calls with the commitment-based close ensure the highlights of the conversation are understood, establish the next point of contact between the buyer and seller, and gain a commitment from the prospect to progress the sale.

Follow-up Confirmation Letters

Once specific actions have been decided, such as an appointment date or follow-up phone call, send a letter to confirm the agreement. The confirmation letter will remind the prospect of commitments, and/or agreed upon dates and times.

> **Note:** Follow up letters should always be sent after a successful cold call—without exception.

Confirmation letters increase the probability of a buyer fulfilling agreed upon commitments (such as showing up for an appointment). They also enhance the credibility of the seller. Potential buyers are impressed when they receive prompt responses, thank-you notes, and reminders. It's an indication of the professionalism and service they can expect in the future should they purchase the good or service.

Not only is it important to send prompt follow-up letters, it is equally important to promptly send any information that you promised to send the buyer. Remember that the sooner it gets there, the fresher your conversation is in the mind of the buyer and the more quickly the sale can be continued.

When emphasizing the importance of follow-up letters at our trainings, participants inevitably ask if sending a follow-up email message is sufficient. My answer is "No." I recommend sending both an email and follow-up letter. In this era of email, there is something professional and satisfying about receiving a follow-up letter, personal note, or thank-you card. It conveys going the extra mile as well as communicating professionalism.

> **Caution!** Confirmation letters should not be more than one page. Keep written communication as brief and to the point as possible.

Sample Follow-up Confirmation Letter

April 9, 2006

Mike Ricks
Director of Sales
World Alliance
25 North State Street
Cupertino, CA. 84629

Dear Mike,

It was a pleasure to speak with you today. I'm pleased we had the opportunity to briefly discuss some of the ways in which Patrick Henry & Associates can be of service to World Alliance.

Enclosed is a brochure that introduces our services. For a more in-depth look at Patrick Henry & Associates prior to our appointment, please visit our Web site, www.PatrickHenryInc.com, which has more information regarding our trainings, technology, and services.

I look forward to meeting with you at 9:20 A.M. on the 20th of April at your facility.

Best regards,

Zac Fenton

Zac Fenton
Account Executive
Patrick Henry & Associates, Inc.
Phone: 1 (877) 204-4341
zfenton@PatrickHenryInc.com

part four

IV

RULES OF ENGAGEMENT

CHAPTER 19

The Role of Credibility in a Prospecting Call

———✦———

Shortly after George Washington's victory at Yorktown, Benjamin Franklin, an ambassador for the United States, attended a dinner of foreign dignitaries in Versailles. The French minister proposed a toast to King Louis XVI, comparing him to the moon. The minister of Great Britain, in like manner, proposed a toast to King George III, likening him to the sun. Benjamin Franklin then stood up and toasted "George Washington, Commander of the American armies, who, like Joshua of old, commanded the sun and the moon to stand still, and they obeyed him."

Few figures in world history have earned or deserved the respect and admiration given to George Washington. He was the Commander-in-Chief of the Continental Army and the first President of the United States. He was also a surveyor, planter, and soldier, but, above all else, he was a man of great integrity.

In the end, what distinguished George Washington from the ordinary man was not his towering intellect or great military genius. It was his character.

———✦———

Credibility Matters

People evaluate not only the content of what a person says, but also the character and trustworthiness of the person saying it. As Stephen R. Covey expresses in *The 7 Habits of Highly Effective People*, "It is character that communicates most eloquently... In the last analysis what we are communicates far more eloquently than anything we say or do. We all know it. There are people we trust absolutely because we know their character. Whether they're eloquent or not, whether they have the human relations techniques or not, we trust them, and we work successfully with them."[1]

It's really no different in sales. As I discussed in Chapter 8, buyers form immediate impressions about sellers. They determine whether or not sellers sound intelligent or ignorant, professional or pushy, even forming a mental image of what sellers might look like. Yet, of all the impressions they make, none is more critical to the success of the seller than credibility because it is the most important judgment buyers make.

Credibility is the impression people form about you, your company, and your product or service. It's a sense of believability, trustworthiness, and perceived competence, and it resonates from your voice, your language, and your tone.

There are two reasons credibility is important to successful prospecting:

1. *Credibility helps establish salespeople as consultants rather than biased product "pushers."* Credibility is a prerequisite to any buyer-seller relationship and forms the foundation of long-term relationships. The key to building effective relationships in any sales situation is establishing credibility early in the selling process.

2. *Credibility sells.* The greater the credibility of the seller, the more value prospects attach to the information presented. Without credibility, buyers won't trust the motives, intentions, or recommendations of sellers. In any sales situation, credibility must be firmly established for the sale to advance. Sellers who don't create credibility won't make it to the investigation stage of the sales cycle.

---

1. Stephen R. Covey, *The 7 Habits of Highly Effective People.* (New York: Simon and Shuster, 1989) 22.

Unfortunately, establishing credibility appears to be easier than it really is. Buyers are automatically suspect of the intentions of sellers. If a buyer feels a seller has less than forthright motives for making the sale, the credibility of the seller is diminished and so is the likelihood for making the sale.

> **Note:** Sellers are subject to Napoleonic Law—guilty until proven innocent. Most buyers are automatically suspect of salespeople. Sales professionals must overcome this stigma by establishing credibility early in the sales call.

The Buyer Method

Buyers consistently evaluate five things when deciding on a particular product or service, normally in this precise psychological order:

1. The sales representative
2. The company
3. The product or service
4. The price
5. The value

The first evaluation buyers make is not about a product or service, it is about the salesperson. Outside of purchasing shelf products from retail stores, the first thing buyers instinctively do is size up the sales representative.[2]

I received a cold call from a salesperson in New York who attempted to sell me financial services. Within thirty seconds of the call, I ascertained I was dealing with a dishonest person. His tone was synthetic and phony, and his use of manipulative, closed-ended questions gave me an immediate, distasteful impression of his character. As a sales professional, I always take cold calls. Unfortunately for him, he earned

---

2. The buyer method is discussed in detail in Chapter 6 of *Sales-Side Negotiation*.

The Buyer Method

Buyers consistently evaluate five things (typically in this order):

The Sales Representative	Honesty, character, attitude, knowledge, experience, etc.
The Company	Reputation, dependability, status, size, stability, etc.
The Product/Service	Quality, features, capabilities, functionality, etc.
The Price	Rates, fees, charges, costs, affordability, etc.
The Value	Benefits, gains, worth, utility, importance, consequences, risks, etc.

Figure 19.1

the distinction as the first salesperson I've ever cut off and said, "Never, ever call me again."

What did this guy do to invoke such a harsh response from a person willing to listen to just about any cold call on Earth? He oozed with duplicity, projecting an image and impression that lacked character. He seemed slimy. He asked me how my family was doing despite the fact this was the first time he had ever spoken to me and had never met my family. He attempted to corner me with closed-ended probes designed to get me to tell him my annual income. When I refused to take the bait, he began telling me I could trust him, that he was my friend. Since this guy was a classic "what *not* to do" case study, I wish I had tape-recorded his call to use as an example of how *not* to cold call.

What was interesting was that this guy never got to the point where he could tell me about his services. For all I knew, he had the most incredible financial services on the planet. He might have been able to make me millions of dollars, but the quality of his goods and services didn't matter because without building trust and credibility, he never made it to the point where he could actually explain what he did that was of value to me. Without trust, I had no confidence in his proposed product or service.

There is nothing intrinsically wrong with engaging in conversational discussions about non-business related issues such as the weather, sports, etc. However, early in the sales call small talk should not dominate the conversation. While small talk and conversational "chit-chat" might seem more comfortable to the seller, it can sometimes smack of insincerity if it's not quickly turned into "big talk." Effective sellers cordially get down to business.

> **The Point?** You validate your trustworthiness by who you are, not necessarily by what you say. The kind of person you are sends loud and clear signals to people. It is communicated on an intuitive level, but it does communicate.

Character

It is character and honesty that give life to professional prospecting skills. Without sincerity and character, potential clients interpret prospecting techniques as manipulative and duplicitous.

One key to success in sales is motivating people to like and trust you. You have undoubtedly heard the oft-repeated selling adage, "People buy from people they trust." A person with character is a person who can be trusted. Far too often this simple reality is overlooked. *In the initial stages of the sales cycle, too many sellers focus on selling their products instead of selling themselves.*

Recipients of sales calls need to feel that sellers are honest and trustworthy. If sellers use manipulative prospecting tactics or pushy cold calling techniques, buyers won't trust them. If sellers sound like oily opportunists, or if they sound phony or insincere, doing anything that indicates a lack of character or integrity, buyers won't trust the seller's motives or recommendations. Without trust in the seller's character, there will be little-to-no confidence in the value of the proposed solutions or disseminated information.

Early in the sales cycle, buyers make quick assessments about the honesty, character, and experience of sellers. Prospective buyers typically decide within the first sixty seconds of contact whether they trust the seller enough to proceed to the next level of the selling process. This is especially true when selling over the phone.

> **The Point?** The most important assessment buyers make surrounds trust and character. "Am I dealing with Vinny the back slapping, plaid-jacketed, used-car salesman trying to sell me a pink Yugo, or is this someone I can trust?"

Industry Related Knowledge

Industry related knowledge is the second component of sales related credibility. In order to establish credibility, sellers need to demonstrate in-depth industry knowledge and utilize correct terminology as it relates to the buyer's business. When sellers don't display adequate industry or market knowledge, buyers feel uncomfortable advancing the call and accepting recommended proposals or solutions.

What if I told you I am a big fan of tennis? You have no reason to doubt it. For all you know, I was once a professional tennis player. You would probably believe me, right? What if we were conversing about tennis and I said to you, "Wasn't that great when Andre Agassi came back after being down four to nothing?" Now do you believe that I'm a huge fan of tennis? For those of you familiar with how tennis is scored, you will quickly see that I do not know what I am talking about.

Sellers not only communicate their level of industry related knowledge with language, they also communicate expertise with conversational content because words, language, questions, and comments reflect the level of experience a person has in any particular industry.

Familiarizing yourself with appropriate market terminology is mandatory. By studying product literature and memorizing key words, concepts, and market specific phrases, sellers enhance their ability to establish credibility early in the sales call.

With telephone selling especially, the person doing the selling must be knowledgeable about the product, market, and/or customers he is contacting. Salespeople need to be able to answer questions, address objections, and provide detailed information about the proposed product or service as it relates to the prospect's interests.

I once heard a salesperson say, "I don't know crap about my product, but I can sell the crap out of it." I was astonished at his false bravado and lack of character. If he didn't know anything about his product, how could he honestly and effectively communicate capabilities of value to buyers? He couldn't.

Demonstrating industry-specific knowledge is crucial to establishing credibility just as understanding industry needs and using market specific terminology indicates expertise that will be of value to buyers.

Testimonials

In our trainings, I frequently ask participants, "How many of you provide buyers with testimonial letters to support the success of your products and services?" I am always amazed at how few hands go up. And yet, what better evidence can a seller have than a statement by a satisfied customer? When sellers attempt to build credibility and provide buyers with evidence that validates product or capability claims, what better proof can a seller offer than a testimonial?

A testimonial is nothing more than a type of evidence. In a court of law, witnesses are called to testify to the truthfulness of certain facts or disputed claims. Client testimonials serve a similar purpose by illustrating how the proposed product or represented business has benefited other companies and organizations. Used appropriately, testimonials communicate similar benefits available to the targeted audience.

Testimonials are extremely powerful and help build the credibility and reputation of the salesperson, company, product, price, and value of the offering.

The Point? Establish credibility early in the sales call by projecting character, demonstrating industry and product related knowledge, and providing buyers with client testimonials.

CHAPTER 20

Cold Calling Behaviors to Avoid

⟞⟐⟝

Thomas Edison was fiercely competitive. Some would even say maniacally competitive. In 1889, one of Edison's competitors, Serbian scientist Nikola Tesla, appeared to have succeeded in creating an electrical system based on an alternating current (AC). Edison viewed the AC current as a competitor to his own invention, direct current (DC). Envious of Tesla's creation, Edison decided to ruin his competitor's reputation by making the public believe that the AC current of electricity was dangerous, unsafe, and irresponsible. To prove his point, Edison captured an untold number of household pets and electrocuted them to death with an AC current. When this failed to sway the public, he convinced the New York state prison authorities to use the AC current to conduct its first execution by electrocution, but to the shock of the authorities (pun intended), the AC current was not strong enough and only half killed the man, so the procedure had to be repeated. It was an awful scene and the credibility of Edison was damaged far more than Tesla's.

The mistake that Edison made was "charging in" without giving due consideration to the consequences of his actions. His reckless arrogance and cold competitiveness led to one of the most embarrassing episodes of his life.

⟞⟐⟝

The Five Prospecting Behaviors Buyers Despise

Like Edison, many salespeople fail to adequately consider the consequences of their behavior. They just pick up the phone and start dialing for dollars without giving due consideration to the methods and techniques they are using.

There are many annoying or irritating behaviors that can lead to lost sales. However, there are five specific behaviors buyers despise most about sales calls. Each of these five behaviors should be completely avoided:

1. Long-winded sellers
2. Cold calls that sound canned
3. Being interrupted
4. Sloppy pronunciation
5. Sellers with inadequate product or service knowledge

Long-winded Sellers

There are few things worse than taking a call from a long-winded seller. Long-winded sellers talk themselves out of sales every day. When sellers blabber on and on, buyers grow irritated and annoyed. Even if they are interested, buyers worry that the time it will take to maintain a relationship with the seller may exceed the value of the proposed good or service.

Sales Calls That Sound Canned

People have developed immunities against canned cold calls. No one likes to talk to an automated human being. There is a natural resistance to sales calls in general, but especially to calls that sound like the caller is reading. As soon as buyers recognize callers are reading directly from a script, they find a way to get off the phone.

To avoid sounding canned, be yourself. Be sincere, genuine, and personable. Let your natural personality communicate to the buyer. Remember that people like dealing with people, not corporations, not brand names, and certainly not robots.

Successful sellers avoid sounding canned and obviously scripted.

Being Interrupted

Immature and inexperienced sellers believe that talking is more important than listening. How often have you been interrupted by a salesperson excited to tell you about a product or service? How often have
sellers put the beginning of their sentence in the middle of yours? It's
highly disrespectful and irritating. When sellers consistently interrupt
buyers, they lose sales. The product or service may be terrific, but it
doesn't matter because once interrupted, buyers feel annoyed and even
manipulated by sellers. Remember, *telling is not selling*.

> **Note:** When buyers talk, listen. Don't interrupt.

Sloppy Pronunciation

There is a clear connection between the quality of a salesperson's speech
and the perceived quality of the product or company being represented.
When sellers use slang, poor language, or sloppy pronunciation, prospects (rightfully so) interpret these to mean that the seller is ignorant,
uneducated, undisciplined, or careless.

I received a call from a person selling long distance services. I am
certain that she offered a terrific service, and I'm sure I would have
learned about it—if I had been able to understand her. During the call,
I kept interrupting her saying, "What did you say?" or "Say that again
please?" I finally hung up the phone and thought to myself, "What
idiot hired that person to make cold calls?" She was probably a great
person, but it didn't matter because her enunciation was so sloppy and
slurred that I could not understand her.

As previously mentioned, when I talk about appropriate pronunciation, I am not talking about accents. Accents, in fact, are interesting
and lead to conversations about national origin, travel, vacations, trips,
countries, etc. Accents are interesting, but sloppy pronunciation is not.
When I refer to sloppy pronunciation, I am talking about slang, lazy
speech, incomplete sentences or incorrect diction such as, "you guys,"

"we was," "ya know?" etc. The issue is carelessness.

If you are serious about making successful prospecting calls, use clear language and avoid sloppy pronunciation.

Sellers with Inadequate Product or Service Knowledge

Prospects who are intrigued by opening cold call statements often ask sellers preliminary questions about their company, goods, or services. In a way, prospects reverse qualify sellers by asking questions that ensure it is in their best interest to continue the conversation.

Whether you are selling mortgage loans, high tech software, or life insurance, adequate product or service knowledge needs to be demonstrated. We have all been put on hold by sellers who could not answer fundamental product or service related questions. Not only is it time consuming for both parties, it is unprofessional and irritating.

It's an undeniable fact that you cannot prospect well if you do not have adequate product or service knowledge. You have to know what you are selling and how it benefits customers.

If you lack product knowledge, study printed material, marketing collateral, or ask for company training. Do what it takes to learn and demonstrate adequate product knowledge so that you don't waste the time of the prospect and undermine your selling opportunity.

> **The Point?** Avoid the aforementioned cold call behaviors like the plague. They are the fastest ways to sink your opportunity to sell.

CHAPTER 21

Measuring Success

You will miss 100 percent of the shots you never take.

—Wayne Gretzky

———◆———

In 1202, Leonardo Fibonacci published *Liber Abaci*, in which he introduced to Europe what we now refer to as Arabic numerals (even though the Arabs borrowed the numerals from India). This simplified system offered a great advantage over the clumsy Roman numerals, which were difficult to add and subtract and which virtually defied multiplication and division. The introduction of Arabic numerals eliminated the need for the abacus, a manual computing device consisting of a frame holding parallel rods strung with movable counters. With the Arabic numeric system, merchants could calculate the new numbers more easily in their heads or on paper.

The introduction of the Arabic system was not without controversy. Universities, government, and religious authorities expressed suspicion of the new numbers because they originated from "infidels." In stubborn defiance, many European universities continued using the abacus and Roman numerals. The merchants, however, could not afford to wait for the approval of professors and priests. They needed a practical means of calculation and immediately began using the Arabic system.

The new numbers proved to be practical and spread quickly throughout the commercial centers of Europe, producing a mathematics revival, which helped clerks, bankers, and merchants perform the tasks of converting money, calculating interest, and determining profits and losses.

———◆———

Selling: a Numbers Game

To maximize selling success, it's important to grasp the relationship between numbers and results. Like the ancient merchants of Europe using Arabic instead of Roman numerals, sellers who grasp the relationship between measurement and performance have a distinct edge over competitors who don't.

We have all heard the saying, "Selling is a numbers game." Despite this clichés overuse, it is true. Measuring activity, success, and rejection rates gives sellers the statistical averages to determine the number of sales calls they need to make to achieve financial objectives.

It is no secret that most salespeople don't like maintaining numerical data or creating reports. However, the pros of reporting far outweigh the cons of not keeping score. In fact, without reporting, it's impossible to consistently achieve peak performance standards.

By closely monitoring prospecting activity results, sellers establish prospecting schedules based on factual data. By determining the number of calls it takes to eventually close a sale (call to close ratio), sellers can evaluate how much time they need to cold call each day to meet personal goals, sales quotas, and financial expectations.

Know Your Numbers

Cold calling is a ratios game. If you know your ratios, you can adjust selling focus and efforts accordingly. If you don't know your numbers, how will you know whether or not your sales approach is working?

> **Note:** Tasks that are measured are accomplished. Tasks that are not measured are forgotten. You can only expect what you inspect. Keep score.

In order to know your numbers, answer the following questions:

- *How many cold calls do you need to make each day to reach your sales goals?*

• *How many dials does it take to talk to a decision-maker?*
• *How many calls does it take to set an appointment or qualify a lead?*
• *How many appointments or qualified leads do you need to close a sale?*
• *What is the average dollar amount of each sale?*

By maintaining accurate prospecting statistics, you can adjust sales strategies, fine tune sales plans, and make needed changes to cold call approaches. Knowing your numbers allows you to understand your prospecting strengths and weaknesses. Armed with this data, you can make intelligent modifications to your selling behaviors.

To measure the success of your prospecting efforts, get in the habit of tracking five vital statistics:

1. *The number of dials:* How many times you dialed phone numbers over a specified period of time (day, week, month).
2. *The number of completed calls:* Actual discussions with prospects.
3. *The number of objective successes:* The number of set appointments or qualified leads.
4. *The number of sales:* Actual purchases that resulted from cold calls.
5. *The average amount of each sale:* The combined average of total sales.

> **Note:** Use *The Weekly Prospecting Report* (Figure 21.1) to quantify the relationship between dials, completed calls, successes, number of sales, and sales amounts.

Calculate Your Daily Cold Call Quota

I was once given a territory with an expected quota of $500,000 in gross sales over a 12-month period. The average sale was about $20,000, so based on the average sale amount, I knew I needed to make 25 sales to reach my quota. At the time, this particular sales organization was closing about 20 percent of their appointments—in other words, about one in five. I knew that I needed to set at least 125 appointments to close enough sales to hit my quota of $500,000. Cold calling was the primary method for setting appointments, and they typically set one appointment for every 20 calls made.

- Quota: $500,000
- Average sale amount: $20,000
- Required sales to reach quota: 25
- Average appointment close percentage: 20% (1 in 5)
- Needed number of appointments: 125
- Number of appointments set per cold call: 5% (1 in 20)
- Needed number of calls over a 12-month period: 2,500
- Needed number of cold calls a day to hit quota: 10

Based on these numbers, I calculated that I needed to make 2,500 hundred calls a year to meet my quota of $500,000. That averaged 10 cold calls a day if I worked 250 days a year (not a mammoth task by any means). Of course, meeting my quota was not my goal. I wanted to surpass my quota, so I set aside one hour a day for cold calling in order to make at least 20 calls a day to exceed my quota—which I did.

Why Keep Score?

By utilizing a consistent tracking system, sellers can identify exact numbers to measure return on investment ratios. Armed with performance data, they can determine areas that need improvement, establish appropriate prospecting schedules, and make accurate revenue projections.

An added benefit of reporting is building confidence. When sellers can review a sales report that reflects productive selling statistics, it builds certainty and eliminates doubt.

The Point? Using statistics from prospecting reports, sellers can measure the number of cold calls it will take on a daily or weekly basis to achieve quota standards and sales goals.

Power Prospecting Weekly Report

Name: Week:

Date	Dials	Completed Calls	Successes	Number of Sales	Avg. Sale Amount

Total:

Total Sales	
Total Dials	
Sales/Dial	
Commission Rate	
Commission/Dial	

$$R.O.I. = \frac{(Total\ \$\ Sales)}{(Time\ Invested)}$$

Figure 21.1

CHAPTER 22

The Ten Commandments of Cold Calling

—————⊰•⊱—————

As a child in Egypt, Moses was saved from the slaughter of all male Israelite children by being hidden in the bulrushes in the Nile where he was found by one of Pharaoh's daughters and raised in the Egyptian court. He later became the prophet and lawgiver of the Israelites and led them out of Egypt. After wandering in the wilderness for forty years, the Israelites approached the promised land of Canaan.

In an attempt to communicate with God, Moses climbed Mount Sinai. There, Jehovah gave him the Ten Commandments for the Israelites to keep in order to maintain their favorability with God. Throughout their history, when the Israelites obeyed the Ten Commandments, they flourished, but when they disobeyed the Ten Commandments, they floundered.

—————⊰•⊱—————

Similar in principle to the original Ten Commandments (in a purely contextual sense), *The Ten Commandments of Cold Calling* are rules of engagement. They are proven success formulas and tested prospecting principles that lead to success. By following *The Ten Commandments of Cold Calling,* sellers achieve predictable sales results. By violating *The Ten Commandments of Cold Calling,* sellers proceed at their own risk.

Commandment 1: Develop a Spontaneous Tone

People do not react well to calls that sound dull, boring, or as if they are coming from a machine, so develop a positive, spontaneous tone that establishes believability and genuine rapport between the buyer and seller. Monotone calls drain the life out of cold calls and encourage prospects to terminate the conversation. Calls that sound artificial project shallowness and scream, "Inexperienced, gum smacking, minimum wage telemarketer!"

Be upbeat, positive, and enthusiastic. Sound human and natural to establish cold call chemistry. Even when reading from a script or using an outline, use an upbeat, conversational approach. Practice good telephone skills, and you will maximize your selling efforts. If necessary, use a tape recorder or telephone message machine to record cold calls to review and improve delivery skills. Do whatever it takes to develop a spontaneous tone.

Commandment 2: Get Down to Business Early in the Sales Call

Far too often salespeople try to initially engage buyers with small talk about sports, weather, golf, or other non-sales related items. While momentary small talk is perfectly acceptable (and in some cases even preferable), don't over do it. Sellers who chit chat about non-business related issues too long run the risk of sounding phony and insincere.

> **Note:** Small talk is good—in small doses. Big talk is better. Get down to business early in the sales call.

While engaged in small talk, avoid controversial topics such as religion, politics, and sex. People have an amazing amount of stored up energy (and sometimes frustration) with regard to social and political topics, so even casual remarks by a seller can set off a powder keg response from a buyer. Sellers are better off avoiding controversial topics completely.

Commandment 3: Avoid Delivering Premature Presentations

Remember not only to say the right thing in the right place, but far more difficult still, to leave unsaid the wrong thing at the tempting moment.

—Benjamin Franklin

———⟶❧⟵———

During World War II, the British Intelligence agency assembled Britain's finest mathematicians and chess players to crack the German communication code. These mathematical and mechanical geniuses deciphered a predecessor to the modern computer, a machine called *Enigma*. The first intelligence Enigma deciphered was information concerning a massive bombing of Coventry, England. British Intelligence was suddenly placed in a precarious dilemma. If they scrambled extra forces to meet the attack, the Germans would be alerted that their code had been broken. On the other hand, if they did not muster a defense, thousands of people in Coventry would be killed. Winston Churchill and other British leaders decided that to achieve long term military objectives, it was necessary to allow the attack to proceed unimpeded. British leadership was forced to exercise almost unbearable patience as they watched the town of Coventry bombarded into rubble.

———⟶❧⟵———

Like British military leaders during World War II, cerebral sellers do not sacrifice long term objectives for short term advantages. They avoid the temptation to rush in and share all the information they possess about the benefits and capabilities of their product or service.

One of the most common mistakes sellers make on initial sales calls is jumping into premature solution presentations. Solution presentations should be reserved for face-to-face meetings or later in the sales cycle, not in the initial cold call because premature presentations can potentially bore a buyer, create unnecessary objections, or kill the sale early in the prospecting stage. Premature presentations bring up features and capabilities without first identifying correlating needs, pains, and problems. As a result, questions, obstacles, and objections are sometimes introduced that have to be overcome later in the sale. In addition, too much information can confuse or overwhelm a prospect.

Of course, product and service capabilities need to be introduced to prospects, but in the initial sales call, delivering an introductory presentation and asking questions should be the focus of the presentation.

Commandment 4: Concentrate on Discovery-Qualification and Need-Problem Questions

Good sellers focus on fact-finding and qualification questions early in the sales relationship. *The DNASelling Method's* first step is asking discovery-qualification questions (see Chapter 11). These questions are critical to the success of the qualification-based cold call.

Discovery questions help identify information that can be used to make informed proposals and accurate recommendations. Once a salesperson has obtained discovery information, prospects should be qualified. Qualifying questions determine if prospects are worth pursuing. The remaining steps of *The DNASelling Method* are based on information gained from discovery-qualification and need-problem questions.

Note: Remember, no problem = no sale. Focusing on need-problem questions in the initial stages of the sales call will ensure you address the needs, issues, and interests of the prospect.

Commandment 5: Avoid Exaggerated Statements and Rhetorical Questions

In most cases, sellers set the tone of a sales conversation. If the seller sounds cordial, professional, and positive, normally buyers will respond "in kind." If you want a quality response, have a quality opening statement and avoid exaggerated statements and bizarre questions such as, "If I could save you millions of dollars, would you be interested?" Most people feel insulted and manipulated when they are asked questions like that.

Opening statements that use wild exaggerations to gain attention come across as eccentric. Avoid opening cold calls with over used hyperboles that begin with "ultra," "mega," "awesome," "incredible," "amazing," "remarkable," and other superlatives prospects have heard a thousand times before.

Like exaggerated statements, prospects do not respond well to rhetorical questions, so avoid using questions such as, "Is productivity important to you, Mr. Nugent?" "Is quality important to your business, Mrs. Liddy?" Or, "Would you like to increase your sales?" Of course productivity, quality, and increased sales are important to buyers, and it's insulting to have to state the obvious. Prospects immediately recognize rhetorical questions as manipulative and self-serving.

Eccentric openings don't work because they produce eccentric responses. From the beginning of the sales process, be professional. Avoid exaggerated statements and rhetorical questions.

Commandment 6: Be Organized

I managed a salesperson who had a wonderful personality, excellent sales and presentation skills, and a great sense of humor, but he lost winnable sales because of his lack of organization. He lost leads and phone numbers. He miscalculated travel times between appointments and was often late for presentations.

I worked with him on a major account that involved hundreds of thousands of dollars. We ran into a small emergency and needed to contact the primary decision maker instead of the project coordinator.

It was a Saturday morning and we had a problem that needed to be addressed immediately, but even though personal and business contact information for this decision maker had been provided, our salesperson had lost the information. He was so unorganized and had so much paper and so many piles of folders and trash on his desk that the phone number had been lost in the clutter. We failed to contact the decision maker, and, as a result, missed a fantastic sales opportunity.

It would be difficult to exaggerate the importance of being organized. Unorganized sellers are less successful than organized sellers. Without an organized means of tracking sales leads, sellers duplicate calls, misplace names, lose phone numbers, and lose sales.

Use a contact management system to keep track of calls (see Chapter 3). Record detailed notes for follow-up calls, emails, and letters. A computerized system allows sellers to easily access contact records and facilitates the sales and prospecting process.

Regardless of whether you use an electronic or paper system, you should implement a lead tracking system to be organized.

Commandment 7: Make an Appointment with Yourself to Cold Call for One Hour Each Day

The 80/20 rule is a fundamental business principle, equally applicable in sales. Top sales performers spend 80 percent of their time selling and servicing their customers and set aside 20 percent of their time for prospecting. Scheduling time for cold calling decreases the peaks and valleys of selling. Elite sellers make appointments with themselves each day to make uninterrupted cold calls. Making an appointment with yourself to cold call for one hour a day (without interruption) allows you to constantly generate qualified opportunities without getting burned out.

> **Note:** Prospect between the hours of 9:00 A.M. and 10:00 A.M. (buyer time).

I recommend prospecting between the hours of 9:00 A.M. and 10:00 A.M. (buyer time) five days a week. This hour is sometimes referred to as "The Golden Hour of Selling." According to The American Telemarketing Association, a person is five times as likely to reach a prospect during these hours than at any other time of day.

Commandment 8: Use a Telephone Headset

When I cold call, I prefer to use a telephone headset because I like to stand up when I make my calls. Not only do headsets free my hands up for taking notes or typing, they also allow me to walk or move while cold calling. Additionally, because I am standing up, my voice resonates, my energy is higher, and my mind is more alert. Headsets help me multi-task with focus. By freeing up one of my hands, I am more capable of utilizing cold call resources such as notepads, automation programs, and script sheets.

Headsets also make cold calling more comfortable by reducing stress in shoulder and neck areas. Headsets are readily available and make sense for sellers serious about cold calling. Use a telephone headset.

Commandment 9: Have Achievable Expectations

The power prospecting model is not designed to work 100 percent of the time. The goal is to improve call-to-close ratios (sometimes referred to as a "hit" ratio) and increase call-to-sale percentages.

Far too often sellers are pumped up about cold calling only to become discouraged due to unrealistic expectations. Even Babe Ruth, the greatest big league hitter in the history of baseball, was not successful a majority of the time. The greatest salesman on Earth is not going to hit sales homeruns the majority of the time, so don't set yourself up for failure. Have realistic, achievable expectations when cold calling.

To keep things in perspective, and to maintain a positive attitude, I recommend that every now and then you just *blow one for fun*. "Hello, does someone there speak Swahili? We're doing a survey but only to people who speak Swahili." Or, "We're selling security certificates that are specifically designed for three-year olds. Can I speak to your three-year old please?" Have fun. Lighten up. Understand that losing a few battles is a part of winning the war. Have realistic expectations.

Commandment 10: Judge Yourself by Your Successes, Not Your Failures

Cold calling can be rough on a salesperson's ego, but rejection is part of the sales game. It's like being drilled in a football game by a middle linebacker. It doesn't happen every play, but every now and then it's bound to happen. Remember that rejection comes with the turf and is a natural part of the sales profession. You are not alone. Every salesperson worth his or her salt has been knocked in the dirt a few times.

Early in my career, I lost a major sale. Not only was I personally disappointed, but I had to report the loss in a sales meeting in front of my colleagues and managers. I was embarrassed. After the meeting, the president of the company pulled me aside and said, "Patrick, you win some, and you lose some. The key is to judge yourself by your successes, not your failures."

His words had a great impact on me. Although I had lost a large sale, on the whole, I was doing extremely well.

The important principle to remember is to *learn from your losses, but focus on your successes.* There are going to be days when you don't qualify a lead, set an appointment, or make a sale. But if you stay at it, your successes will far outweigh your failures.

In Summary

The Ten Commandments of Cold Calling are:

1. Develop a spontaneous tone.
2. Get down to business early in the sales call.
3. Don't jump into a premature solution presentation.

4. Concentrate on discovery-qualification and need-problem questions.
5. Avoid exaggerated statements and rhetorical questions.
6. Be organized.
7. Make an appointment with yourself to cold call for one hour each day.
8. Use a telephone headset.
9. Have achievable expectations.
10. Judge yourself by your successes, not your failures.

CHAPTER 23

Implementing Power Prospecting Principles

It behooves every man to remember that the work of the critic is of altogether secondary importance, and that, in the end, progress is accomplished by the man who does things.

—Teddy Roosevelt

———❦———

Peter the Great was the most influential czar and military leader in Russian history. At the age of seventeen, he became the reigning monarch of Russia and quickly determined that his country did not compare favorably with other European powers. Having assumed the throne of a country that missed both the Renaissance and the Reformation, Peter was determined to improve the cultural, scientific, and military status of his country. In 1697, he traveled throughout Europe under a pseudonym and without his royal trappings. He studied shipbuilding in Holland and England and observed the military practices of Prussia. During his travels he visited schools, factories, museums, military academies, and arsenals. Upon his return to Russia, he summoned Western educators, businessmen, sailors, and military personnel to serve as his advisors and to train his people in their respective skills. He built a new capital city, St. Petersburg, to serve as a window to the west and demanded that education, trade, and industries incorporate Western ideas and methods. He simplified the Russian alphabet, introduced Arabic numerals in commerce, and provided for the publication of the first newspaper in his country. In his efforts to Westernize Russia, he went so far as to demand that all men shave their beards and wear western clothing in the kings' court.

Not since the efforts of Alfred the Great in Britain had a nation's leader gone to such efforts to modernize and improve his country. The czarist Russia Peter left when he died survived as a European power for two centuries. Its ultimate demise came not from a foreign power, but from the internal Bolshevik Revolution in 1917.

Peter the Great is an extraordinary example of a person who was willing to pay the price to succeed. He recognized that his country needed to improve, and he made the necessary reforms to make it happen. He not only studied the advanced scientific and cultural practices of the west, he implemented them. He took action. Although the changes were difficult, and at times costly, they paid off. His reforms eventually placed Russia on equal footing with Britain, France, and Prussia.

From Principles to Practice

At the conclusion of our sales trainings, I am consistently asked, "How do we implement your training? How do we convert principles into practice? Is there a way for us to turn board room trainings into practical application?"

There is, of course, no easy answer to these questions. Understanding does not necessarily translate into *doing*. However, there are some fundamental guidelines that will speed up the implementation of power prospecting principles.

Once individuals have mastered the ideas and concepts of *Power Prospecting*, it is critical to channel the newly acquired information into habits.[1] I have identified five implementation rules that follow skill-learning principles:

- Focus on one skill at a time
- Focus on quantity, not quality
- Set goals and standards
- Plan
- Don't become discouraged

---

1. *Patrick Henry & Associates* has systematized an implementation program that can be customized to the needs of individuals and organizations. To learn how to best implement power prospecting skills and strategies for your business or situation, contact *Patrick Henry & Associates* at 1 (877) 204-4341.

Focus On One Skill at a Time

———➤●《———

In 890, Alfred the Great identified "seven maxims" he strove to follow. He then worked on each behavior individually. Benjamin Franklin did much the same in 1771. He outlined thirteen virtues that "occurred to me as necessary or desirable" and set aside time to focus on each virtue separately. "I determined to give a week's strict attention to each of the virtues successively. Thus, in the first week my great guard was to avoid every day the least offense against temperance [his first virtue]... Proceeding thus to the last, I could get through a course complete in thirteen weeks and four courses a year. And like him who, having a garden to weed, does not attempt to eradicate all the bad herbs at once... but works on one of the beds at a time, and having accomplished the first proceeds to the second."[2]

———➤●《———

Basketball coach Pat Riley outlines in his book *The Winner Within* a program that he used with the Los Angeles Lakers to break down complex skills into component behaviors. "From a list of fifteen possible measures, we selected five that had really cost us the last championship. These defined five 'trigger points,' five areas which comprised the basis of basketball performance for each role and position. We challenged each player to put forth enough effort to gain just one percentage point in each of those five areas."[3] Riley then focused on each skill, one at a time, with each player. The next year, the Lakers won the NBA championship.

---

2. *The Autobiography of Benjamin Franklin* (New York: Barnes and Noble Books, 1994) 106-108.

3. Pat Riley, *The Winner Within* (New York: Berkley Books, 1993) 163.

When softball players work on hitting, they don't attempt to work on their throwing skills at the same time. They focus on one skill at a time. Like successful athletes, successful negotiators do not work on multiple skills simultaneously. They isolate a particular skill and work on it. After mastering the targeted skill, they move on to the next skill.

> **The Point?** Focus on one skill at a time and hammer it. Work on it. Think about it. Write it down. Practice it. Concentrate on developing one skill at a time.

Focus on Quantity, Not Quality

As a young man, I had a basketball coach teach me how to shoot free throws. He showed me the correct mechanics of shooting—bringing my elbow up to a square position, bending my shooting wrist back, following through, etc. After teaching me the correct way to shoot, he then said, "Now go shoot 100 free throws and come back and talk to me again." He understood quantity would lead to quality.

Patrick Henry & Associates refers to this skill-learning concept as *The Quantity Principle. The Quantity Principle* instructs students to focus on skill quantity versus skill quality. New behaviors are learned through a quantity of repetition and practice. Quality comes with time. As new behaviors are learned, adjustments will be made, and skills will be refined. The important part of learning a skill is doing, practicing, engaging.

> **Caution!** In the initial stages of skill learning, don't worry about perfection. Don't worry about making mistakes. Don't worry about quality. Focus on *quantity* and quality will follow.

Set Goals and Standards

A goal is a desired objective used to motivate and enhance a person's ability to succeed. Goals give people direction and focus and are essential to improving performance.

Setting and achieving goals is not a trivial process. It takes good data, good thinking, and good instincts to set good goals. Inappropriate goals can actually have an adverse effect on a person's performance. Unrealistically high goals that are not achievable not only fail to motivate, they actually discourage people by making them feel unsuccessful. Goals that are too easy to achieve, on the other hand, do not inspire people to stretch and grow.

For example, a seller who wants to improve his or her selling skills can set a goal to memorize two questions from each category of *The DNASelling Method* or create a cold calling script to improve his or her initial presentations. By setting goals, sellers motivate themselves to improve their selling skills and behaviors.

The most important aspect of a goal is its means of fulfillment. After establishing a goal, it is necessary to create a game plan to accomplish the goal. Why? Without clearly identifying steps of achievement, people don't have goals—they have hopes.

A *goal* is an objective; whereas, a *standard* is a means of achieving the objective. Goals without standards are like weight loss programs without exercise. An example of a *goal* is to lose twenty pounds. An example of a *standard* is to workout every morning from 6:30 to 7:00. Standards are like "mini goals" fulfilled on a daily or weekly basis that map a clear path to achieving a goal.

When setting goals, a salesperson should set personal standards to achieve the goals.

The Point? Develop goals and standards that are challenging, motivating, and achievable.

Plan

You've undoubtedly heard Benjamin Franklin's oft-repeated maxim, "By failing to prepare, you are preparing to fail." This dictum is scripture in the business world. Plan ahead. Specify what dates, times, and accounts you will implement your new skills.

In order to sell well, you must first plan well. Strategic planning is the cornerstone of successful selling. If you don't have an effective plan for selling, any success you experience is purely accidental. Use the tools provided in this book to plan your sales calls in advance. Anticipate possible problems or potential resistance. Create cold calling scripts. Plan and analyze the implementation of your newly acquired skills and knowledge. Evaluate your sales calls.

- What went well?
- What could I have done differently?
- Which questions had the greatest influence?
- What mistakes did I make?
- What skills could I have implemented?

The key to implementation is to plan and schedule. Map out what you feel you need to work on. Week one: Creating a Unique Selling Proposition. Week two: Asking better discovery-qualification questions, etc.

Don't Become Discouraged

A smooth sea never made a skilled mariner.

—English Proverb

In 1832, Abraham Lincoln lost his job in a failing business partnership. Also in 1832, he was defeated for the state legislature. In 1833, a private business failed. Although elected to the state legislature in 1834, he implemented an internal improvement project that nearly bankrupted the State of Illinois. He was defeated twice for the house speaker position in 1836 and 1838. In 1843, Lincoln was defeated for the nomination to the U.S. Congress. Although elected to congress in 1846, he lost the renomination in 1848. In 1849 Lincoln ran for a land-office position and lost. In 1854 he was defeated for the U.S. Senate. In 1856, Lincoln was defeated for the nomination for Vice-President, and, in 1858, he repeated his losing bid for the U.S. Senate. In 1860, he was elected President of The United States of America.

Achieving excellence is a journey, not a destination. It's a voyage wrought with bumps and bruises. As Abraham Lincoln's experience illustrates, bouts of failure are part of the path of success. Setbacks and mistakes come with the terrain. It's part of the process. The key is to learn from mistakes and failures and take the lessons to heart.

> **Note:** Most sales are made after the fifth call, and most salespeople quit after the first, so stick with it. This is simply the law of the harvest: As ye sow, so shall ye reap.

Many professionals learn new and better ways of presenting but don't convert the newly acquired knowledge into habits because they become discouraged. Give new skills a chance. No new skill feels natural the first time you use it. It may initially feel a bit awkward and artificial. That's perfectly normal, so don't quit after only a few attempts. Keep working on it. Role-play it, think about it, practice it. Don't become discouraged.

Prospecting Success–Deserve It.

There never has been devised, and there never will be devised, any law which will enable a man to succeed save by the exercise of those qualities which have always been the prerequisites of success — the qualities of hard work, of keen intelligence, of unflinching will.

—Teddy Roosevelt

Prospecting success must be earned. There is no magic potion. In order to be successful, sellers must pay the price by sowing before they reap. They must deserve success.

Cerebral sellers follow a simple success equation:

Power Prospecting Skills x Work = Success

Goals cannot be wish lists. They have to be work lists. Thinking about your dreams is rarely enough to create the habits to fulfill them. While it is good to start with dreams and goals, before any of your dreams and goals can be realized, you must first deserve your success by acquiring selling skills and working hard. By combining old-fashioned work habits with power prospecting skills, you will be equipped with the tools to consistently win.

If you want to succeed—deserve success.

"No one can guarantee success in war—one can only deserve it."

—Winston Churchill

The Point? You can do it. Be "patiently persistent," and your skills will improve. Persevere and your selling success will increase. Follow *Power Prospecting* principles, work hard and you will be successful. You will have earned it.

The SONAR Selling System

The SONAR Selling System is a comprehensive selling process and development curriculum that implements contemporary prospecting, selling, presenting, and negotiating skills. Coupled with effective lead generation and CRM technology, *The SONAR Selling System* equips individuals and organizations with the skills, strategies, and technology to fill pipelines with qualified leads and win more sales.

The SONAR Selling System is a holistic sales and marketing approach validated for helping sales professionals and organizations achieve optimum performance. Based on the philosophy that selling is a science, an observable, verifiable, and measurable process, *The SONAR Selling System* equips clients with the skills, strategies, and technology to increase sales, measure results, and accurately forecast revenue projections.

The SONAR Selling System is the only comprehensive and fully integrated sales performance development model available. Each skill process works seamlessly with others through shared approaches, language, and technology. Sales professionals and organizations trained in *The SONAR Selling System* improve performance, outperform competitors, and increase bottom-line profitability.

Patrick Henry & Associates

Patrick Henry & Associates is a performance development company that coaches individuals and companies to dramatically increase sales revenue.

Each skill related component of *The SONAR Selling System* has an associated book and integrated performance-based curriculum designed for personal, corporate, and executive trainings.

Corporate Training

Patrick Henry & Associates offers the following training programs:

Power Prospecting teaches a structured process for script development, pipeline management, and telephone interaction to generate new leads, set appointments, and fill pipelines with qualified opportunities.

The DNASelling Method provides a systematic approach to selling that improves questioning skills, differentiates presented solutions from competing products, and gains commitment with effective closing strategies.

Winning Presentations instructs business leaders and salespeople in a five-step process *(The Presentation Pedigree)* to prepare strategic content, master effective communication skills, and deliver exceptional presentations.

Sales-Side Negotiation trains business executives and sales professionals to build, balance, and maintain power, recognize and overcome negotiation tactics, minimize discounts, negotiate favorable agreements, and develop mutually beneficial relationships.

Each module of *The SONAR Selling System* has a corporate training program with a one to two day initial training, followed by a structured field application process. An optional one-day mastery workshop is conducted after field application for follow up, skill reinforcement, and permanent change.

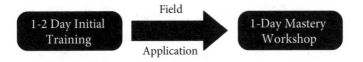

Executive Retreats

For account executives, managers, directors, vice presidents, presidents, CEO's, and other business leaders, *Patrick Henry & Associates* offers executive retreats. Using "train the trainer" methods, *Patrick Henry & Associates* instructs business leaders in *The SONAR Selling System* and equips them with the skills and strategies to incorporate *The Selling System* in their own business or sales organization.

Executive retreats are conducted at prestigious locations around the world and include afternoon and weekend options of fly-fishing, golfing, skiing, hiking, biking, sightseeing, and other recreational activities.

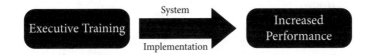

Speeches and Seminars

Patrick Henry & Associates provides speeches and seminars that can be customized to specific audiences, companies, or industries. For more details concerning public seminars, key note speeches, corporate trainings, and executive retreats that teach, train, and certify sales professionals, managers, and executives in *The SONAR Selling System*, contact:

Patrick Henry & Associates, Inc.
1831 Fort Union Blvd. Suite 210
Salt Lake City, Utah 84121
www.PatrickHenryInc.com
1 (877) 204-4341

Selected Bibliography

Adams, Jeremy, Wick Allison, and Gavin Hambly. *Condemned To Repeat It.* New York: Penguin Books, 1998.

Ambrose, Stephen E., *Undaunted Courage.* New York: Simon & Schuster, 1996.

Axelrod, Alan. *Elizabeth I, CEO.* New York: Prentice Hall Press, 2000.

—. *Profiles in Leadership.* New York: Prentice Hall Press, 2000.

Bailey, Thomas, and David Kennedy. *The American Pageant.* Lexington: Heath and Company, 1991.

Beyer, Rick. *The Greatest Stories Never Told.* New York: HarperCollins, 2003.

Boyd, Katherine, and Bruce Lenman. *Larouse Dictionary of WORLD HISTORY.* New York: Chambers Harrap Publishers, 1993.

Corvisier, Andre. *A Dictionary of Military History.* Translated by Chris Turner. Cambridge: Blackwell Publishers, 1994.

Federer, William. *America's God and Country.* Coppell: Fame Publishing, 1994.

Ferris, Timothy. *Coming Of Age in The Milky Way.* New York: Doubleday, 1988.

Franklin, Benjamin. *The Autobiography of Benjamin Franklin.* New York: Barnes & Noble Books, 1994.

Freiberg, Jackie, and Kevin Freiberg. *NUTS!* Austin: Bard Press, 1996.

Greene, Robert, and Joost Elffers. *The 48 Laws of Power.* New York: Penguin Books, 2000.

Hicks, Laurel, and George Thomas. *World History and Cultures.* Pensacola: A Beka Book, 1985.

Jacobson, Julius H., *The Classical Music Experience.* New York: Sourcebooks, 2002.

Laycock, George. *The Mountain Men.* New York: Lyons & Burford Publishers, 1996.

Moore, Pete. *E=MC².* London: Friedman/Fairfax Publishers, 2002.

Novaresio, Paolo. *The Explorers.* New York: Stewart, Tabori, & Chang, 1996.

Ritchie, W.F. *Celtic Warriors*. Buckinghamshire: Shire Publications, 1997.

Scott, McNair R. *Robert The Bruce*. New York: Peter Bedrick Books, 1989.

Sun-tzu. *The Art of War*. Translated by Ralph D. Sawyer. New York: Barnes & Noble Books, 1994.

Warner, Philip. *Famous Scottish Battles*. New York: Barnes & Noble Books, 1996.

Weatherford, Jack. *The History of Money*. New York: Three Rivers Press, 1997.

Index

From Great Moments in History

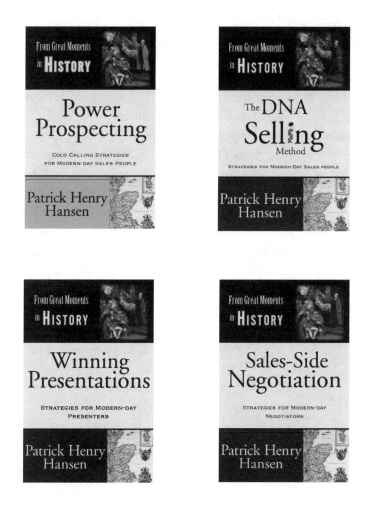

To order the complete *From Great Moments in History* series call

(877) 204-4341

or visit

www.PatrickHenryInc.com

About The Author

Patrick Henry Hansen is the founder of *Patrick Henry & Associates* and is the creator of *The SONAR Selling System, The DNASelling Method,* and *SONAR* technology. His organization provides CRM/consultation, corporate trainings, and executive retreats for sales managers, coaches, and leaders. Mr. Hansen is the author of numerous books and is considered one of the foremost authorities on prospecting, sales-side negotiation, and business strategy. Mr. Hansen is a popular speaker, consultant, and educator, and has trained, coached, and influenced thousands of professionals in *Power Prospecting Principles.*

Prior to starting *Patrick Henry & Associates,* Mr. Hansen was a sales representative, manager, and executive. As an executive for multiple technology companies, he introduced advanced selling systems that increased sales more than 100% in each company.

Mr. Hansen founded *The Business America Radio Show,* received his BA from Brigham Young University and currently resides in Salt Lake City, Utah with his wife Laura and their five children.

Refer questions to:

Patrick Henry & Associates, Inc.
1831 Fort Union Blvd., Suite 210
Salt Lake City, Utah 84121
Phone: 1 (877) 204-4341
Fax: 1 (877) 204-4341
www.PatrickHenryInc.com

From Great Moments in History **Book Series ($19.95 each)**

\# of copies

_____   *Power Prospecting*: Cold Calling Strategies for Modern-day Sales People

_____   *The DNASelling Method*: Strategies for Modern-day Sales People

_____   *Winning Presentations*: Strategies for Modern-day Presenters

_____   *Sales-Side Negotiation*: Strategies for Modern-day Negotiators

_____ S/H   Add $4.00 for shipping & handling (up to 4 books)

_____ Tax   Sales Tax (Utah Residents 6.25%)

_____ Total

Name: _____

Company: _____

Business Address: _____

City, State, Zip: _____

Phone: _____

email: _____

Payment: Cash ____ Check ____ Charge ____ (MasterCard, Visa or American Express)

Acct. # _____

Expiration Date: _____

Signature _____

Please make your check payable & return to:

Patrick Henry & Associates
1831 Fort Union Blvd. STE 210
Salt Lake City, Utah 84121

Call your credit card order to: 877-204-4341 or order online at:
www.patrickhenryinc.com